Landscaping Projects

SIMPLE STEPS

TO ENHANCE YOUR HOME AND YARD

TIME
LIFE
BOOKS

ALEXANDRIA, VIRGINIA

TIME LIFE

HOW-TO

Landscaping Projects

Introduction

Nature may paint her landscapes with broad brush strokes, but beautiful home landscapes are created from a series of small projects. Like pieces of a puzzle, these projects eventually come together to form an attractive, functional whole. The landscaping projects in this book will help you beautify your yard piece by piece, while also helping you shape its overall design.

Creating attractive scenes within your yard is but one aspect of landscape improvement. You will also want outdoor space that is comfortable and enjoyable to use and does not require constant maintenance. Many of the projects in this book focus on transforming problem areas into places that are beautiful, functional, and pleasing to your own personal tastes. Since no two yards are exactly alike, each main project is followed by alternative ideas that may offer a better fit for your particular site, your climate, or for a vision you may have for your home landscape. In addition to these alternative concepts, you can use the plant guides to find the best trees, shrubs, vines, and flowers for the growing conditions in your yard.

Whether you are tackling a problem area such as a slope or turning a shady spot into a relaxing outdoor room, take the time to study a project all the way through before you actually begin the work. Step-by-step photos and instructions guide you through each project, so that any novice gardener or carpenter can complete them successfully. You do not need a green thumb, building expertise, or exotic tools to create raised beds or turn an eroded strip of lawn into a stone walkway. As with the other projects in this book, all you really need to complete them successfully is a willingness to try. ❧

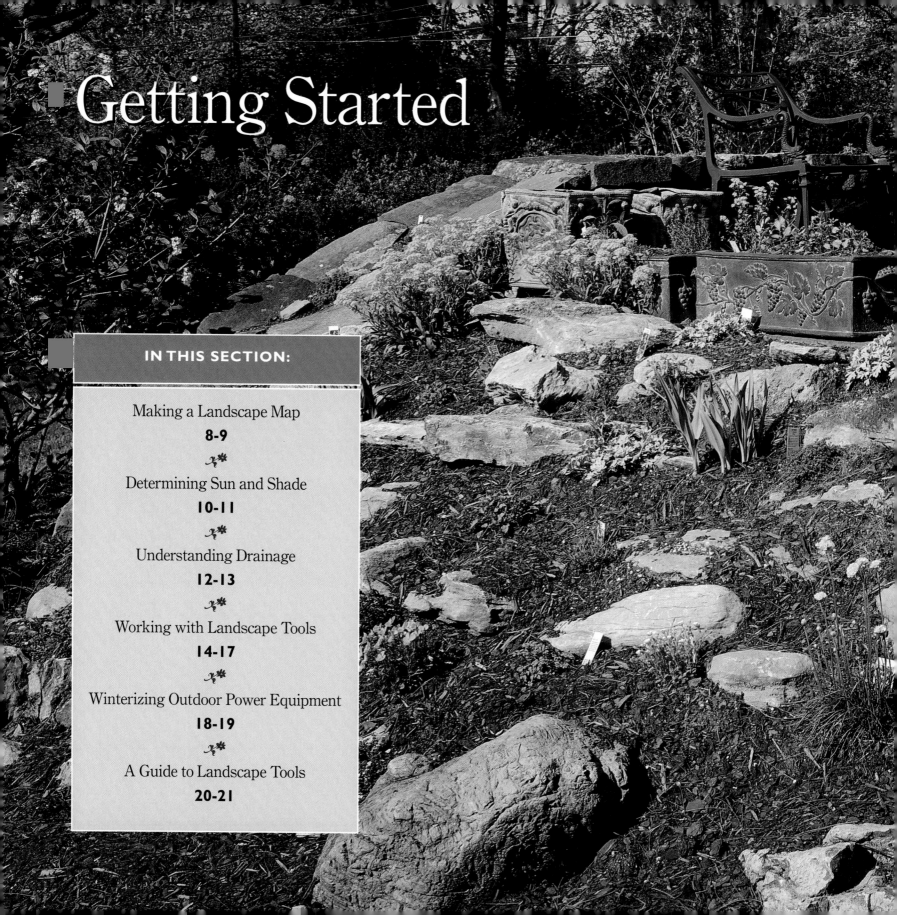

Getting Started

Within your yard there are probably several different microclimates. Perhaps the west and south sides are sunny and open, the north side is shady, and the east side is somewhere in between. This section will help you get to know the unique sites that exist within your yard in terms of light and water, and show you how to work within that natural framework to improve your landscape. As you get to know your landscape better, you will probably discover spots that need only a little work to make them more attractive, along with problem areas that need extensive changes to make them more comfortable, livable, and fun.

Each project you undertake to improve your landscape will be more successful and safer if you use the proper tools. Before delving into specific projects, review the tool basics in this section. You will learn how to choose tools that match your landscaping job, as well as how to store and care for your tools and lawn-care equipment.

As you try different projects, you will learn about gardening, carpentry, masonry, and landscape design. If the skills required to do a certain project are new to you, allow extra time to study the step-by-step instructions. All of the projects in this book are simple enough for beginners, yet so practical that experienced carpenters and gardeners will find them rewarding. ❧

Making a Landscape Map

A landscape map is like the blueprint for your home, giving you a bird's-eye view of every element. A map of your house and all the features of your property is an indispensable tool that allows you to try various plans on paper before deciding on the right one.

Start with a base plan and use overlays (tracing paper sketches that lie on the base plan) to consider any number of landscape factors: sun and shade patterns, prevailing wind direction, drainage patterns, and ideas for plantings. Spending the time and effort to make a comprehensive survey of your landscape will familiarize you with your property, help you envision it over the long term, and aid in avoiding costly mistakes and surprises.

If you have a site plan or property survey, it will contain dimensions. If not, you will need to measure the perimeters of your property, and then draw them as the outer boundaries for your plan. If you plan landscaping changes near your property's boundaries, you will need to obtain a legal survey to avoid potential misunderstandings with neighbors or conflicts on zoning or rights of way.

Make your site drawing to scale. Depending on the size of your property, use the largest scale you can fit on your paper—1 inch to 1 foot, for example. The larger the scale, the easier it will be to work with your drawing. With a scale drawing you'll see at a glance how much space there is for a planting between your hedge and deck, for example, or if an arbor will fit between your house and garage.

Use tracing paper overlays to draw design options to compare and combine. In this way you can try different ideas without having to redraw your map each time.

Consider how you will use your landscape. Keep in mind that service areas should be easily accessible yet hidden from view or attractively screened. Be sure water is close to high-maintenance gardens. Locate children's play areas away from your prize roses. Plant trees and large shrubs where they will have enough room to grow. Consider that a young tree might grow to shade an area that is now a full-sun garden, or that a hedge or fence can be advantageously placed for privacy or as a windbreak. And don't forget how your property will be seen from inside your home. A beautiful view of your yard and gardens from your dining room or a favorite easy chair provides an additional pleasure through all four seasons of the year. 🌿

HAVE ON HAND:

▶ Property survey

▶ 50-foot tape measure

▶ Graph paper

▶ Tracing paper

▶ Pencils

▶ Straightedge ruler

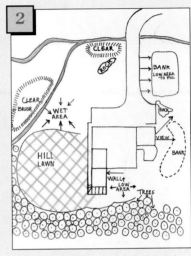

Draw a master plan of your property on graph paper. Show buildings, utilities, driveways, and paths.

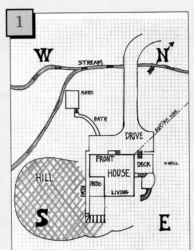

Lay tracing paper over plan and draw existing features: good views, large trees, hedges, large boulders.

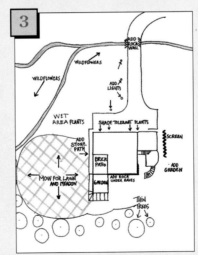

On a second overlay sheet, draw in what you wish to plant: gardens, shrub borders, hedges, and trees.

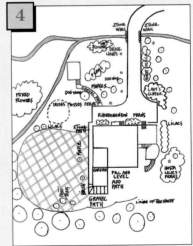

Continue creating and modifying overlays until you are satisfied with your final landscape map.

Determining Sun and Shade

Match plant choices to the light conditions around your house for healthy, vigorous plants that will enhance your landscape. Shade-loving plants become scorched and dried out in too much sun, and sun-loving plants—most vegetables and flowers—become pale and leggy and won't bloom where there is too little sun. Most plants in garden centers carry tags indicating their light requirements. A plant labeled full sun needs at least 6 hours of direct sun per day to thrive. Partial sun means 4 to 6 hours of direct sun, and shade means less than 4 hours of sun per day.

Remember that the path of the sun, as it moves across the sky from east to west, changes during the year. A spot that is shady in the low-angled light of winter may be brightly lit in summer.

Southern exposures receive the most sunlight. Easterly exposures provide gentle morning light. Westerly exposures give hot, strong light in the afternoon. A northern exposure is the shadiest for your plants.

You can let more light into shaded areas by carefully removing lower branches on trees. Orienting beds and rows of plants on a north-south axis, with tall plants to the north, will prevent plants from shading each other. 🌸

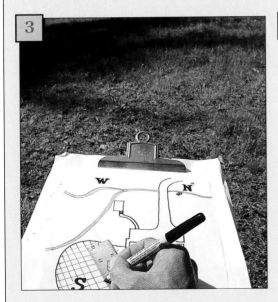

Examine your yard for areas of deep shade, such as north-facing sides of buildings or below large evergreens and trees with dense leaves.

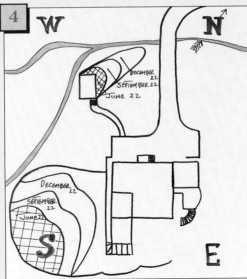

Note locations that get dappled or filtered light through overhanging tree branches. Also note areas of morning or afternoon sun and shade.

Sketch shady areas on a tracing-paper overlay of your site map. Check areas at 2-hour intervals for an entire day to verify sun exposure.

Review your shade map at different seasons to see how the sunlight for each area changes as the path of the sun in the sky changes.

HERE'S HOW

USE SHADE TO ADVANTAGE

Plants require less frequent watering in shady and partially shady areas. In very hot climates, even plants that require full sun may grow better with light afternoon shade, as it helps keep them from wilting or drying out in intense afternoon heat. In climates where low winter temperatures and high winds are the rule, afternoon shade in winter may also reduce scorching of broad-leaved evergreens such as rhododendron. In areas with cool summers, many partial-shade plants can tolerate some sun.

Understanding Drainage

Good drainage is essential for most plants. It allows water and nutrients to reach plant roots, then gets the excess out of the way. Roots will eventually rot where garden soil stays soggy. Good drainage is important for your home as well. Water that collects around foundations can cause flooding and cracking, or can promote rotting wood.

Standing water results from variations in slope or from an impermeable soil layer that prevents water from draining. In most cases, drainage problems can be easily corrected with hand tools. If severe drainage problems exist, or if water collects around foundations, you'll want to employ the services of a professional to regrade an entire area or install underground drains.

Small-scale drainage problems are often the result of compacted soil, usually from heavy foot or equipment traffic. To correct this condition, dig soil at least a foot deep, incorporate a 2- to 3-inch layer of compost, and redirect traffic or install paving over well-used paths.

A few plants, such as willows, some irises, and Japanese primroses, prefer constantly damp soil. Rather than correcting soil drainage, create a garden for moisture-loving plants (see Designing for a Wet Site, page 76).

In spring, observe where standing water collects in your yard; note where it remains for more than an hour after a heavy rain in any season.

If poor drainage occurs in lawns, break up soil with a spading fork, work in compost, and regrade area to even out low spots; reseed.

HERE'S HOW

KNOW WHEN TO REGRADE

Wait until all standing water has drained and the soil has dried out slightly before digging or regrading, because working wet soil will only make it more compacted. To test whether soil is ready, dig up a handful and squeeze the soil in your palm. If it feels wet and forms a sticky lump like modeling clay, wait a few days and test it again. When the soil feels moist and forms a clump in your palm that crumbles fairly easily, it is ready to be dug.

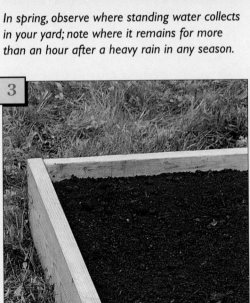

If you wish to plant a garden in an area with poor drainage, build a raised bed. Add enough topsoil or compost to elevate soil 3 to 4 inches.

If an area stays moist year round, consider going natural and converting the spot into a wet garden, using plants that thrive with poor drainage.

Working with Landscape Tools

CHOOSING TOOLS

The proper tools can make each landscape project you undertake turn out just right. The tools needed to complete most landscaping projects in this book are also used to cultivate your lawn and garden. Building projects utilize several common carpentry tools, and maintaining the special landscape features you create may also require some different ones. Smart shopping will make your investment in tools pay off nicely and improve the quality and safety of your landscaping projects.

Whether you're shopping for a hammer or a lawn mower, always handle a tool before you buy it. Match it to your size and strength, and compare tools of varying weights. Carefully inspect handles, blades, and any movable parts to make sure they are perfect. Power tools are a special challenge; they feel different when they are turned on. Shop at stores that provide demonstration mowers you can push or string trimmers you can try for size.

Consider the various uses for each new tool you buy. Find out about warranties, and check on the availability of local repair service and replacement parts. And remember: The first step in using any new tool is to read the instruction booklet from start to finish. ✺

CLEANING TOOLS

The last step in any landscaping project is to clean and put away your tools. Digging tools, like your shovel or post-hole digger, may rust if damp soil is left clinging to the blades, and the rust will weaken the metal. When cleaned and oiled twice a year, the wood handles on rakes and shovels will stay strong and be less likely to develop splinters. Use a soft utility brush to remove dirt and mud from wood handles.

Let them dry before wiping with linseed oil, or any oil used to polish wood furniture.

Clean carpentry tools work better than dirty ones, and they will last longer, too. Deposits of dirt and dust on carpentry tools can make it difficult to read measurements, which may lead to costly mistakes. You can prolong the life of your power tools by keeping their air intake vents clear of dust and debris. When air cannot flow freely into an engine or motor it can quickly overheat, which may cause permanent damage to its internal parts.

Keep a collection of clean rags handy for cleaning and drying your tools, but dispose of rags that become soiled with oil or other flammable substances. Make sure they are wrung out and put them with your solid waste. Recycle your thin cotton towels and old T-shirts. They make great shop rags since they are both soft and absorbent. ❧

HAVE ON HAND:

- ▶ Wheelbarrow or tub
- ▶ Water
- ▶ Regular vacuum with hose attachment, or hand-held rechargeable vacuum
- ▶ Several clean rags
- ▶ Soft utility brush
- ▶ Linseed oil

You can clean several digging tools at once by washing them in a wheelbarrow or tub filled with water.

Vacuum dust and dirt from carpentry tools, and then wipe them clean with a damp cloth.

Brush or vacuum debris from the air intake vents on power tools after each use.

Rinse your cleaning rags and let them dry so they will be ready when you need them again.

KEEPING TOOLS SHARP

Any tool that includes a blade will work better and require less effort from you if the blade is kept sharp. Shovels, hoes, and pruning tools require periodic sharpening, which you can easily do yourself. However, cutting blades that spin, such as the blades on most lawn mowers and blade attachments for weed trimmers, must be perfectly balanced to limit vibration when the tools are in use. Instead of sharpening these blades yourself, have them professionally sharpened, or

invest in a replacement blade.

The goal of a good sharpening job is to restore the blade to its original condition, which varies with the type of tool. Most shovels and spades have a very slight bevel, or angle, along their sharp edge. Heavy use in compacted or rocky soil can wear the edge so badly that instead of a bevel, close inspection will show a series of nicks along the cutting edge. If you cannot find the original beveled edge on a spade or hoe, assume that the bevel was on the back side of the blade.

To sharpen large tools, you will need a metal file, commonly called a mill bastard file. Thoroughly clean and dry your tools before sharpening to prevent slips. Wear long pants, since you will probably be sitting down and holding the tools with your legs as you sharpen them. Sharpening each tool should take just a few minutes. 🌸

HAVE ON HAND:

▶ Mill bastard flat metal file

▶ Small container of household oil

▶ Absorbent, disposable rag

Sit and hold the handle of the tool between your legs. The bevel should face away from you.

Hold file with both hands. Firmly push outward 30 to 50 times; sweep diagonally against beveled edge.

Give nicks a few extra strokes with the file to make the edge smooth and uniform.

Dot edge with four drops of oil. Wipe with a soft rag to spread oil over the sharpened edge.

STORING TOOLS

Tools are easily lost, as everyone who has ever worked with them knows. However, you will rarely lose even the smallest screwdriver if you make a habit of returning your tools to their proper storage places when you have finished using them.

You will want to keep your tools in a weatherproof area, but, no matter where you store them, a large tool collection will take up less space if you hang most of your tools.

And long-handled tools, properly hung up, will not fall where you might trip over them.

A toolbox or cabinet is a good storage place for small carpentry tools. Lightweight plastic toolboxes are now widely available at hardware stores. Some have wheels that make it easy to roll them to where you're working. Keep power tools, such as drills and circular saws, protected from dust and safely out of reach of children. You will need childproof storage space for any flammable or poisonous substances such as lubricants and gasoline. Keep these in clearly marked containers made for such storage.

At the end of a project you may have a few leftover nails, bolts, or screws. Save them in small plastic containers to keep them dry and free from rust. Label these containers for quick access whenever they're needed. ❧

HAVE ON HAND:

▶ Pencil

▶ Tape measure

▶ Carpenter's level

▶ One 4-foot-long 1 x 4, of pine or poplar

▶ Small box of 3-inch-long finishing nails

▶ Hammer

Draw a horizontal line on the wall, at least 6 feet from the floor. Make sure the line is level.

Find the wall studs by tapping on the wall and listening for a higher pitch. Mark studs with your pencil.

Position the board on the horizontal line. Nail it in place, driving two nails into each stud.

Drive five pairs of nails 1 inch into the boards. Hang your large tools on these nails, heads up.

Winterizing Outdoor Power Equipment

When your lawn mower, weed trimmer, leaf blower, and other outdoor gas-powered tools are to be stored for more than two months, spend a little time preparing them so that they will be ready when you need to use them again. While you're at it, manual and electric tools will also benefit from your attention before being stored.

Clean dirt and debris from your equipment by washing waterproof parts with warm, soapy water and a soft cloth. Wipe off dust that has accumulated on air intake vents, and remove and clean filters if your tools have them. Before storing any battery-operated tools, fully charge batteries. Then unplug battery chargers, wipe them clean with a damp cloth, and store them in plastic bags once they are completely dry. Your large tools will take up less room in your storage area if you are able to remove or fold down the handles.

Clean and dry the blades of manual reel mowers or lawn edgers; then, to prevent rust, wipe them with a rag that has been lightly sprinkled with household oil. Before putting garden hoses away, drain them. Water left inside will expand as it freezes, which may result in cracked hoses.

GAS-POWERED MOWER

The hour or so it takes to winterize your lawn mower will go a long way toward extending its engine's life, and the same procedures will benefit all other gas-powered tools. Fuel system parts such as tanks, hoses, filters, and carburetors should all be cleaned before storage.

Begin by draining the fuel tank. Put leftover gas in a closed container and dispose of it properly. When the fuel tank is empty, try to start the engine. This should clear the fuel lines and carburetor of any remaining fuel. Use a damp cloth to wipe away oil and dirt that have accumulated on the outside of your mower, paying special attention to air intake vents. If possible, lay it on its side, scrape, then use a strong spray of water to remove any dried grass from the blade and under the deck. This is a good time to inspect the blade for large nicks and to install a new one if needed.

Drain the oil in your mower before you store it for the winter, being careful to dispose of the old oil in an environmentally safe manner. Changing the spark plug as described at right is another way to ensure a fast spring start-up. Finally, cover your mower with a blanket, canvas tarp, or plastic drop cloth to keep it clean. 🌸

HAVE ON HAND:

- ▶ Spark plug wrench or adjustable wrench
- ▶ Tablespoon
- ▶ Fresh engine oil (two-stroke oil for two-stroke engines)
- ▶ Disposable paper or plastic cup
- ▶ Two clean rags
- ▶ New spark plug
- ▶ Canvas tarp or plastic drop cloth

Before changing a spark plug, turn ignition off. Disconnect spark plug, and unscrew it with a wrench.

Place 1 tablespoon oil in paper cup; pour it into the spark plug hole. Plug hole with a clean rag.

Slowly pull the starter handle to distribute the clean oil; allow it to recoil, and slowly pull it again.

Install the new spark plug. For safety, leave the ignition cable disconnected until the tool is used again.

A Guide to Landscape Tools

LAWN

Choose tools that match your lawn-care jobs, to help save time and energy. Follow the safety instructions that come with large power tools.

MOWER
Self-propelled models are safer when mowing slopes. Bag attachments reduce clipping and leaf collection chores; mulching mowers eliminate them. Look for easy-start electric ignition.

STRING TRIMMER
Lightweight electric models are ideal for small yards. Heavier, gas-powered trimmers with blade attachments can handle woody brush and, some trimmers, edging jobs.

DIGGING

Technique can be as important as tools. To ease digging strain on your back, bend your knees and lift with your legs and shoulders.

SHOVEL
Choose handle length and blade size proportionate to your height and comfortable lifting strength. Fiberglass handles are lighter but can be slippery.

MATTOCK
Use pick end for loosening rocky or compacted subsoil. Blade end is ideal for chopping roots and rough compost material. Swing it as you would a miner's pick.

BUILDING

Good tools can last a lifetime if stored in a clean, dry place. For safety's sake, clear your work area of clutter before you begin projects.

TAPE MEASURE
Look for a 1-inch-wide flexible metal tape that retracts into a sturdy box. A 25-foot-long tape with carrying clip is ideal for most projects.

HAMMER
Standard claw hammers with hammer heads come in various sizes, attached to wood handles Try out a few for hand-held comfort before buying.

Occasional Use of Tools

You can rent large power tools if you think you will use them only once. If you enjoy making things, these tools will be good investments. Consider coordinating your purchases with those of relatives, friends, or neighbors so tools can be shared. 🌺

EXTENSION CORD
A heavy-duty, insulated extension cord will last for years. Required features include 3-pronged plugs at both ends and a length of at least 25 feet. Uncoil before using.

LEAF RAKE
Long, lightweight tines are good for raking up leaves and grass clippings. Large rake heads are useful for large jobs, but a smaller head is easier to handle in tight spaces.

LAWN EDGER
Use to groom turf along sidewalks and driveways and to stop grass from creeping into flower beds. Sharpen the blade often and clean thoroughly between uses.

ASPARAGUS FORK
Use to pry out tap-rooted weeds without disturbing surrounding turf. Also known as fishtail weeder or asparagus knife. Handy also for weeding vegetable and flower beds.

POSTHOLE DIGGER
Essential for digging deep, narrow post holes. This tool comes in large and small sizes. The large ones are best only for people who are both tall and strong.

DIGGING FORK
Loosens soil without compacting it. Also useful for moving mulch or aerating soil. The short, strong handle has an end grip designed to facilitate prying action.

WHEELBARROW
Handles many different jobs, such as transporting soil or mulch, mixing small batches of concrete, or moving tools and materials. Models with plastic tubs are light and durable.

CARPENTER'S LEVEL
Bubbles within oil-filled chambers tell you if an object is perfectly horizontal or vertical. Essential for most carpentry projects.

SCREWDRIVER
Basic equipment includes a set of at least four, all with medium-length shanks: a large flathead, a small flathead, a large Phillipshead, and a small Phillipshead.

STEPLADDER
A wood or metal, five-step folding ladder is useful for many building projects, hedge trimming, and tree maintenance on lower branches. Be safe; don't step above third rung.

CIRCULAR SAW
Running an electric saw well requires practice, but it can cut wood faster and better than a manual saw. Always wear safety glasses and ear protection when using a circular saw.

POWER DRILL
Use different bits to make guide holes for nails and screws, to install screws, or to drill holes for dowels. Available in plug-in and cordless models.

Basic Landscaping Projects

The parts of your landscape you use most often tend to be close to the house or along a well-traveled path. Improving those areas by paving walkways with stone or expanding your patio makes outdoor living more enjoyable and adds to the value of your home. Your choice of materials will help set the tone for the rest of your yard. When deciding how you will enclose your planting beds, or when choosing the type of surface for your patio, think ahead to your long-term plans for your landscape so that the different elements will work together harmoniously.

Whether you are installing a watering system or turning a washed-out path into a walkway, take accurate measurements so you can correctly estimate the amount of materials you will need for each project. Heavy lifting is required when excavating soil or working with stone. To prevent possible injury to your back, make lifting with your legs a habit. Take your time with these projects, and set your own pace. You will have less lifting to do if you have mulch, lumber, or other materials delivered close to where they will be used. While large projects are in progress, cover your materials with a plastic tarp to keep them clean and dry. ❧

Installing Drip Irrigation

A drip irrigation system is the most efficient way to water your garden, in terms of both your effort and water use. Drip irrigation systems use a porous soaker hose or, in more expensive systems, a series of delivery hoses attached to emitters that slowly release water at the plants' roots where it is needed. Drip irrigation avoids problems associated with overhead sprinklers, which waste water, require time and effort to move, and can promote plant diseases by drenching leaves.

Install your system in early spring so you are ready to water by the time dry weather hits. Setting the hoses out early in the season saves effort since it is easier to move around in the garden before plants grow big. Also, you can see clearly how to space the soaker hoses for the maximum benefit of all the plants in your garden. If possible, design drip irrigation systems so the soaker hoses can be left in place all season. You may wish to hide the hoses under a loose mulch such as bark chips.

You will probably need one or more ordinary hoses to connect the soaker hose(s) to a distant faucet. Measure the distance from the faucet to the nearest point of each growing area so you can purchase the shortest connector hoses needed. Plan to remove the connecter hoses between waterings if they cross areas of heavy traffic or lawn that needs mowing.

If you wish to run more than one hose from a faucet, purchase a splitter, which attaches directly to the faucet. Each branch of the splitter has its own on- and off-valve, giving you more flexibility.

Another way to enhance your drip irrigation system is by using a timer. The added expense is well worth it if you need to be away or have a tendency to forget to turn off the water. Timers allow you

HAVE ON HAND:

▶ Tape measure
▶ Ordinary garden hose
▶ Soaker hose
Optional
▶ Splitter attachment
▶ Timer

to program the system to go on and off at certain times and for a specific duration without your having to be there. Timers are available at any garden center and come with easy instructions.

The right frequency of watering depends on weather, soil type, and needs of specific plants. The goal is to keep garden soil evenly moist but not soggy. Watch your soil and plants for signals. Puddling and runoff are signs of overwatering. Too much water will cause leaves to yellow and plants to rot. Not enough water will cause leaves to droop.

Water deeply to encourage good root growth. Plants that are deeply rooted are well anchored and better able to withstand fluctuations in temperature or rainfall, and they can reach deep down into the soil to get nutrients. Adjust water pressure until water soaks in slowly rather than runs off the surface. 🌿

Early in spring, measure distance from faucet to garden to find number and lengths of hoses needed.

Attach splitter (and timer) to faucet; connect ordinary hose(s) to lead from faucet to growing areas.

Snake soaker hoses along rows in vegetable gardens and between plants in flower beds and borders.

Attach soaker hoses to connector hoses and test system to be sure it delivers water at the right rate.

Installing a Simple Patio

A properly installed patio located just outside your back door serves as an outdoor room—a place for relaxation, eating, entertaining, and working on projects that are too messy for the kitchen table. As a transition area between the house and the rest of the landscape, a patio has the feel of the outdoors with the tidiness of indoor space.

Determine the size of your patio by considering your available space, its relationship to the scale of your house, and the furniture and equipment it needs to hold. For example, to accommodate a standard picnic table with benches, a barbecue grill, and two lawn chairs with a small table, you will need an area at least 12 feet on each side, or 144 square feet.

Paving slabs of natural or reconstituted stone, plain concrete, bricks, or block pavers can be used for your patio floor. Bricks and concrete pavers are relatively inexpensive to use. When set in a properly prepared bed, they can mold themselves to the slight shifts that develop in the subsoil—common around a new house. When deciding whether to dry-lay your paving materials in sand or stone dust—very fine, crushed gravel—or set them in a concrete base, consider your site, design preferences, and climate. ❧

DRY-LAID BRICK

This 12 x 12-foot patio is large enough for both grilling and dining. The basket-weave pattern shown here is a simple way to position bricks into a smooth surface that drains quickly. If your soil has poor drainage, lay down a bed of gravel before adding stone dust and sand. ❧

HAVE ON HAND:

- ▶ Tape measure
- ▶ Twelve marker stakes
- ▶ Hammer
- ▶ String
- ▶ Shovel
- ▶ Metal rake
- ▶ Stone dust
- ▶ Water
- ▶ Landscape fabric, 12 x 12 feet
- ▶ Four 8-foot landscape timbers and four 4-foot timbers
- ▶ T-square
- ▶ Spikes
- ▶ Carpenter's level
- ▶ Clean sand
- ▶ Kneeling board
- ▶ Bricks, approximately 650
- ▶ Wheelbarrow
- ▶ Broom

Choose site. Hammer two stakes at each corner and three stakes along the outermost edge of each side. Tie string to stakes to create square.

Remove large rocks or other items from area. Use shovel to clear area to a depth of 10 inches. Level the area with a metal rake.

Add a 4-inch layer of stone dust to the excavated area. Distribute with rake to make a level bed for patio. Water thoroughly so it settles.

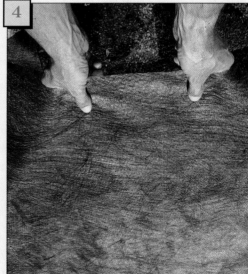

Place landscape fabric over level stone dust. This will prevent weeds from growing up between bricks in the future. Stretch edges to each side.

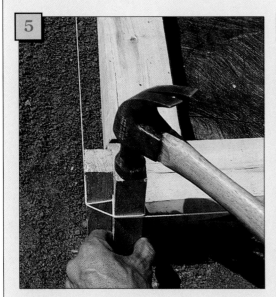

Place a 4-foot and an 8-foot timber along each edge, just inside the stakes. Hammer stakes in so they hold timbers firmly in place. Level area.

Use a T-square to ensure corners are square. Nail corner timbers together with spikes. After all corners are nailed, check with level.

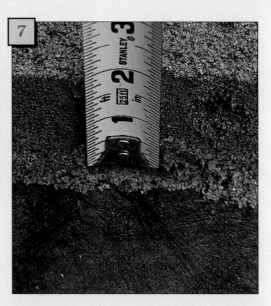

Add 2 inches of clean sand on top of stone dust. Water layer well to settle the sand, tamp and smooth with a rake when dry enough to work.

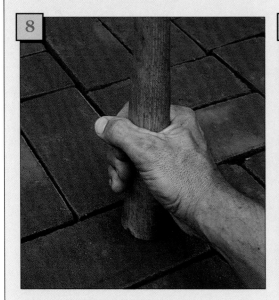

Arrange bricks on top of the sand, tapping into place with a hammer handle. Kneel on a board as you go to avoid making sand base uneven.

Keep the surface of the bricks you are placing even. Use a level to check each section or row and add sand to even surface as needed.

To keep bricks in place and give a finished look to your patio, add a thin layer of sand to patio surface, and sweep to fill spaces between bricks.

Alternatives

INTERLOCKING PAVERS

Interlocking pavers are formed from durable concrete material. They are easy to work with and provide clean, straight edges because they are uniform. Pavers are also very stable, providing a hard, even surface that is easy to clean and to maintain with either hose or broom. Because they are available in a variety of colors and shapes, it's easy to choose a paver that complements your home and garden as well as one that offers an interesting, finished geometric pattern to your patio area. Because of its contemporary look and feel, a surface made with pavers is especially suited to modern surroundings.

Preparation for paver installation is similar to that of brick. If your soil drainage is poor, first put down a level bed of gravel. Then, fit the pavers together tightly and evenly; with the more informal look of brick, this is not as important. Use a heavy rubber mallet to knock on the side of each paver after it is placed. Remember to make sure the crevices between the pavers are uniform for a finished, formal look. ❧

GRANITE

Granite is an excellent natural surface for your outdoor patio. This exceptionally durable material provides a naturally beautiful texture and color and is suitable for use in almost any landscape. Although more expensive than other pavers, granite paving stones are long lasting and easy to maintain; they don't become slippery when wet and they're easy to clean with water or a broom. You can plan a design that is made completely with the same size granite stone or you may want to combine sizes (and even colors) to create a unique and personal look. If you have a stone foundation, consider building your patio up against your house. The patio will then look like a natural and permanent extension of your home.

You can place your granite patio stones on stone dust or concrete with a 2- to 4-inch layer of crushed gravel. Lay it as you would loose bricks, or allow 1- to 2-inch crevices between the stones. Fill these crevices with a mixture of equal parts of sand and weed-free compost and plant with creeping thyme, sweet woodruff, or other small plants with aromatic foliage. In very damp settings, you might also plant plugs of native moss in the crevices. ❧

Installing a Garden Walkway

Establishing a garden walkway will add interest and definition to your landscape. Your walkway might serve as the shortest distance between two well-traveled points, or lead strollers to meander through special parts of your garden. It can also serve as a focal point and be a destination in its own right.

A path directs the way you move through the landscape, serving as a means of traffic control. A well-placed garden path can protect your beds and large areas of ground cover from being trampled. Install pathways to replace or prevent worn tracks in your lawn. If possible, make them 3 to 4 feet wide, so that two people can walk side by side. And consider making your walkway of stone. Stone paths are well worth the effort they take to install as they delight the eye and last for many years.

To enhance the character of a stone walkway, try planting low-growing perennials between the stones. Ground-hugging herbs with fragrant foliage, such as creeping thymes, Roman chamomile, and Corsican mint, are popular choices; they release their delightful scents when crushed underfoot. In moist, shady spots, native mosses are perfect for growing between stones. ❧

FIELDSTONE PATH

Flat pieces of unfinished stone, called fieldstone, are often sold by masonry supply companies. For a walkway 4 feet wide and 20 feet long, plan on using a ton of fieldstone. If fieldstone is not available in your area, you can use the same procedure to install a walkway made of concrete pavers or any type of flat stone. 🌿

HAVE ON HAND:

- ▶ Marker stakes (two per each 3-foot length of walkway)
- ▶ Twine
- ▶ Small sledgehammer
- ▶ Tape measure
- ▶ Fieldstone
- ▶ Shovel
- ▶ Pick or mattock
- ▶ Metal rake
- ▶ Landscape fabric
- ▶ Stone dust
- ▶ Clean, coarse sand

Use stakes and twine to mark outline of walkway. With a sledgehammer, drive stakes into ground at 3-foot intervals along walkway sides.

Measure walkway length and width and multiply to get square footage. Use this figure when ordering fieldstone.

Pile fieldstone or have it delivered as close as possible to site to save extra hauling. The pile may kill grass if left for more than two weeks.

Excavate the soil from the walkway area with a shovel. Remove soil to a depth of the fieldstone's thickness plus 4 inches.

With pick or mattock, remove any large stones you encounter. Smooth excavated walkway with a metal rake so base appears roughly level.

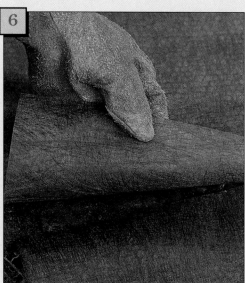

Spread landscape fabric over entire base to keep the walkway free of weeds. To join pieces, overlap edges by a few inches.

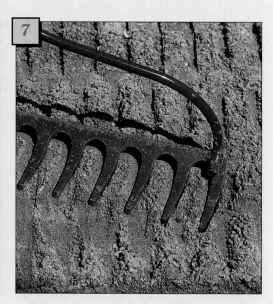

Spread a 3-inch layer of stone dust evenly over landscape fabric. Rake it level. Tamp down and smooth with the back of the metal rake.

On top of the stone dust, spread an inch of clean, coarse sand. Tamp and level with rake to form a firm foundation for your stone walkway.

Arrange all stones on top of the sand. Then use the wooden handle of the small sledgehammer to level each stone and settle it into the sand.

After all the stones are settled in place, fill in the cracks between stones and along the edges with additional coarse sand.

Alternatives

A MULCH WALKWAY

A walkway made of shredded bark mulch or bark chips is ideal for woodland walks, informal garden paths, and utility paths for garden carts and other equipment. Bark is also quiet to walk on and blends nicely with natural surroundings.

A mulch path is quick and easy to install. First, clear the path of eye-level branches and other obstructions. Remove rocks with a pick and rake the area smooth before applying a 3- to 4-inch layer of mulch. Spread mulch evenly over the entire area and rake it smooth. If the path is surrounded by lawn, install edging on either side to help keep mulch in place. Check the depth of the mulch every year and renew as needed.

Several kinds of bark mulch are available either bagged or in bulk from garden centers. Avoid the very large, chunky materials, which make an awkward walking surface. A standard bag of bark mulch is approximately 40 pounds. This amount of mulch can be expected to cover an area of 2 square yards to a depth of approximately 2 inches. To cover a large area, it is more economical to buy mulch in bulk (by the truckload). 🌿

A GRAVEL WALKWAY

Gravel paths are easy and inexpensive to install, and they provide a clean, durable surface that makes a pleasant sound when crunched underfoot. Because gravel packs well, carts and wheelbarrows move easily over it, and its fine texture makes it especially useful for small or narrow places.

Choose a color that blends well with your surroundings. A very pale gravel will look right at home in a desert environment or by the sea, while a darker gravel will look more natural in wooded areas. Choose a gravel diameter smaller than 1 inch for comfortable walking. Small, rounded pea gravel or pea stone makes a particularly nice surface.

Begin by clearing the path of any obstructions. Install landscape fabric to minimize weeds, keep gravel from disappearing into the soil below, and keep it clean. Secure the landscape fabric and keep gravel in place by edging on either side. You can use bricks set on end, treated 2 x 4 lumber, landscape timbers, or commercial edging strips. For maximum longevity, install gravel over a 3-inch base of crushed stone. After applying each wheelbarrow load of gravel, smooth it over with a metal rake. 🌿

Building a Raised Bed

Raised beds, where garden soil sits above ground level, are an attractive addition to your landscape as well as an easy way to solve garden problems. A raised bed allows you to create ideal soil conditions for specific plants, from adequate drainage to the appropriate nutrients. With the right soil in place you can include more plants closer together for a beautiful display or a more productive harvest. In addition, planting can begin earlier since the soil in raised beds warms faster in the spring—a good reason to consider building and filling your raised bed in the fall of the year.

Convenience is another advantage of the raised bed. A 4-foot-wide bed can be planted, weeded, and watered from the bed's perimeter. Soil compaction is avoided, and the loose soil is easy to work. If you are planning to build more than one raised bed, keep wheelbarrow and garden-cart access in mind, and mulch paths between beds with shredded bark or sawdust to keep weeds under control.

Whether your bed contains flowers, vegetables, herbs, or shrubs, match the scale of its plants to the scale of the bed. It will add an orderly and appealing element to your landscape or garden. 🌼

A WOODEN BED

Wooden raised beds are economical, and no special equipment or expertise is needed to build them.

Use air- or kiln-dried lumber where edible plants are grown. Pressure-treated lumber, though more durable, may leach toxic metals into garden soil. Do not use creosote-soaked timbers for edibles.

You may want to drive stakes at set intervals along the bed's exterior to reinforce the frame against soil pressure. ❦

HAVE ON HAND:

- Tape measure
- Four marker stakes
- String
- Garden spade
- Metal rake
- Three 2 x 4s, 8 feet long, one cut in half
- Eight 3-inch wood screws
- Screwdriver
- Four 4-inch L-brackets
- Carpenter's level
- Sixteen 1-inch wood screws
- Wire mesh, 4 x 8-foot piece
- Wire cutters
- Two dozen 1-inch roofing nails
- Hammer
- Soil and compost
- Water

Optional
- Eight stakes, 1 x 1 x 18 inches

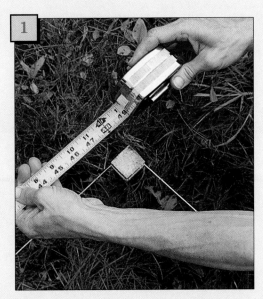

Mark off intended site with stakes and string. Position bed to receive maximum sunlight by orienting long sides north to south.

Remove sod and any large stones from bed area. Till the soil to a depth of 3 inches. Level with back of rake head.

Arrange lumber around bed's edges. Drill pilot holes for 3-inch wood screws. Fasten frame with two screws in each corner.

Reinforce box corners by attaching a 4-inch L-bracket to the inside of each corner using 1-inch wood screws.

Position the box over your site and check to see that it is level. If not, dig shallow trenches at bed perimeter to level it.

Unroll wire mesh. Use wire cutters to remove a 2-inch square from each corner. Fold the 2-inch edges up 90 degrees. Line bed with mesh.

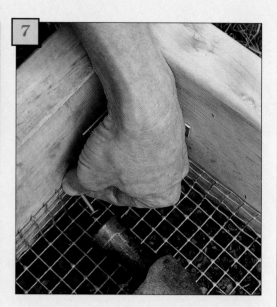

Attach mesh to sides with 1-inch nails at 1-foot intervals. Make sure nailheads overlap mesh. Your bed is now safe from burrowing rodents.

Fill the bed with a mixture of 90 percent soil and 10 percent compost to within 2 inches of the top of the frame. Do not overfill.

Smooth the soil with the back of rake head to create a level planting surface. Water the bed thoroughly to settle soil.

Revisit your new bed the next day and add soil to low areas where settling may have occurred. Water any amended spots before planting.

Alternatives

A TIMBER RAISED BED

Landscape timber, a heavy-duty yet attractive lumber cut to a standard 4 inches by 4 inches, is an excellent choice of material for a long-lasting raised bed. Ideal for jobs where a large amount of soil needs to be supported, it is a vast improvement over the massive, creosote-soaked railroad ties that have been used for raised beds in the past. Landscape timbers are readily available at most home and garden centers.

The sturdy, rustic-looking lumber is easy to stack, making it possible to build your soil to whatever depth you choose. Support, however, is needed to keep the timbers in place over time. As with other wooden beds, you can attach L-brackets to the inside of each corner and drive in wooden or metal stakes along the exterior of the bed to secure the timbers against soil pressure. Better yet, use heavy-duty bolts to fasten the corners.

Building your raised bed with landscape timbers has another benefit. Once your bed is tilled and work in the garden is under way, the timbers' width provides a convenient place to sit, reducing the amount of bending required to plant, weed, and harvest.

A FREESTANDING RAISED BED

The freestanding bed, a raised bed with no built structure to contain it, offers many advantages. It is the fastest and the easiest design to build. In addition, it is the least durable—a distinct advantage when shape, size, and use for your bed may change from one year to another. In a vegetable garden, for example, it's important to rotate types and placements of crops in order to avoid diseases and soil depletion. And if you're not certain you'll like a raised bed in a particular spot, its impermanence makes it the easiest type to move or eliminate.

A freestanding bed could be your best choice if space is limited. You can increase planting area and yield by sowing crops across the top and sides of the bed. Though the sides of freestanding beds will naturally erode from rain and routine watering, a layer of straw mulch will lessen the impact of water hitting the soil surface. Planting the sides of the bed also helps hold the soil.

You can build freestanding raised beds up to a level of 8 inches without having to contain the soil. Keep in mind that these beds are less tidy than other types and should be used where a little soil in the walkways is acceptable.

Edging Your Driveway

THIS GARDEN THRIVES WITH

SUN	WATER	SOIL
Full	**Medium**	**Fertile**

The first part of your landscape that people see is your driveway. Finishing the edge of your driveway with naturally neat plants will make your entire front yard look more polished and will serve practical purposes as well. The soil along driveway edges tends to wash away, but a narrow, mulched border of deeply rooted plants can help prevent this problem. Edging your driveway also helps eliminate the weeds that often grow in the transition area between a lawn and any paved surface.

When designing an edging for your driveway, make sure you allow ample room for people to get into and out of their cars. Also avoid having your edging interfere with traffic patterns or play areas. The end of the driveway closest to the street usually has more room for creative landscaping than the areas closer to the house.

Your driveway edging can be a thin ribbon of a single plant or a narrow bed planted with several different plants in a repetitive pattern. Try to include small evergreens to give the edge form and definition during the winter. Between your cultivated plants and adjoining swaths of lawn, install a strip of hard plastic, stone, or brick edging to stop lawn grass from creeping toward the driveway.

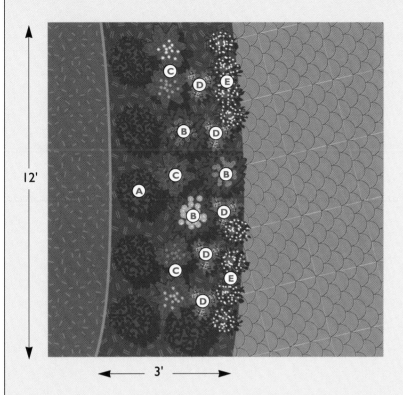

12'

3'

PLANT LIST

A. Edging boxwood, 6, 1-3 feet tall

B. Miniature rose, 3, 16 inches tall

C. Stock 'Brompton Dwarf', 5,
    18 inches tall

D. Pansy, 15, 9 inches tall

E. Sweet alyssum, 8, 6 inches tall

(See next page for more on plants.)

HERE'S HOW

WINTER DE-ICING

In areas with cold winter climates, avoid using driveway de-icing compounds that contain rock salt or sodium chloride. Instead, use those made with calcium chloride or urea, which won't damage edging plants.

1. Remove sod from a 3-foot-wide strip along the driveway. Use a spade to cut horizontally beneath the grass so that 1 inch of soil remains attached to grass roots. Roll up sod in sheets and transplant to another part of your yard. When the sod has been removed, cultivate the soil and work in a 3-inch layer of compost.

2. Plant five container-grown edging boxwoods (A) along lawn side, 2 feet apart. Plant one more, 1 foot from driveway edge, as shown, to establish pattern. Plant miniature roses (B) in a triangular group to become a focal point in the edging bed.

3. Plant stocks (C) 2 feet apart down the center of the bed to form a broken line for the length of the bed.

4. In groups of three, plant pansies (D) 1 foot from driveway side of the bed. Space each group of pansies 30 inches apart to form an irregular line down the length of the bed.

5. Plant sweet alyssum (E) 8 inches apart along the driveway side of the bed. Thoroughly water all plants. Cut a clean edge where the bed meets lawn, and install a hard edging. Mulch the bed with 2 inches of shredded bark or another attractive mulch.

Plants for Your Driveway's Edge

The planting scheme for this driveway edging combines evergreen dwarf boxwoods and miniature roses with annual flowers that are widely available as bedding plants. The stocks and alyssum bring fragrance to the bed, and the pansies help unify the color scheme. Pinks and blues coordinate with the decorative concrete of the driveway, and the white alyssum along the edge is clearly visible at night.

These bedding flowers are cool-season plants that will perform best in climates where nights remain cool all summer. If you live in a warm climate, you could substitute more heat-tolerant annuals, such as dwarf zinnia, portulaca, and ageratum during the summer months, and perhaps use dwarf nandinas instead of the boxwoods. Be sure to place the plants in a repetitive pattern in order to emphasize the continuity of the bed. ❦

EDGING BOXWOOD
Buxus sempervirens '**Suffruticosa**'
1-3 feet tall
Zone 5
Insignificant flowers; glossy green leaves on stiff, woody stems; well-drained, neutral soil; full sun; medium water. Prune spring and midsummer.

MINIATURE ROSE
Rosa hybrid
16 inches tall
Zone 6
Small red, pink, or yellow flowers all season, small, shiny leaves; fertile soil; full sun; medium water. Fertilize in early summer and deadhead to encourage blooms.

STOCK
Matthiola incana '**Brompton Dwarf**'
18 inches tall
All zones
Pink, red, purple, white, or yellow flowers all season; soft green leaves; fertile soil; full sun; medium water. Blooms repeatedly in cool weather if deadheaded. Fertilize monthly.

PANSY
Viola x *wittrockiana*
9 inches tall
All zones
Flowers in many colors and bicolors during cool weather; dark green leaves; well-drained, fertile soil; sun/part shade; medium water. Dies out in hot weather.

SWEET ALYSSUM
Lobularia maritima
6 inches tall
All zones
White, pink or purple flowers spring to fall if cut back periodically; narrow green foliage; any soil, sun/part shade; medium water. Likes cool weather. Feed monthly.

CARE FOR YOUR DRIVEWAY EDGE

SPRING Prune winter damaged twigs from boxwoods and roses. Scatter slow-release balanced fertilizer into soil beneath mulch according to package directions. After last spring frost, set out annual bedding plants: stocks, pansies, and alyssum.

SUMMER Periodically deadhead annuals to promote bushy growth and to encourage repeat flowering. Weed bed as needed, and water deeply during dry spells. After roses finish blooming, cut them back by one-third to encourage repeat blooms.

FALL After your first hard freeze, pull up annuals and compost the plants. Renew mulch to keep the bed looking neat through winter. In cold-winter areas, mulch over the crowns of roses for extra winter protection. ❦

Alternative

PERENNIALS FOR EDGING

You can create a low-maintenance edging for your driveway by using perennial plants such as the ones listed below. Liriope, which is hardy in Zone 6 and warmer climates, is the most popular choice for edging driveways since it is vigorous enough to resist weeds and serve as a barrier to lawn grass, yet very slow to spread to areas where it is not wanted. In shady places, pachysandra works equally well. To link the bed that edges your driveway with the rest of your yard, try to repeat plants or patterns that appear along the driveway in other parts of your landscape.

More colorful perennials for edging include moss phlox, candytuft, and maiden pinks. All of these flowers are long-lived, hardy perennials, but they may need help controlling the erosion that occurs next to driveways when rainwater flows off the edges. Large edging stones next to the driveway may help, as long as they are placed so they won't obstruct winter snowplows.

Areas near your driveway edging should be carefully maintained. To avoid making a driveway feel closed-in on a small lot, install an edging bed on only one side of the driveway, and border the other side with an expanse of lawn. ✿

PACHYSANDRA
Pachysandra terminalis
5 inches tall
Zone 3
Greenish-white flowers not showy; shiny green leaves with scalloped edges; slightly acidic soil enriched with humus; part/full shade; high water.

MOSS PHLOX
Phlox subulata
6 inches tall
Zone 3
Pink, lavender or white flowers, early spring; stiff, needle-shaped foliage; any well-drained soil; full sun/part shade; low water. Tolerates drought. Fertilize in late summer.

EVERGREEN CANDYTUFT
Iberis sempervirens
10 inches tall
Zone 4
White flowers in spring; narrow, dark green leaves on mounded plants; slightly acidic soil; full sun/part shade; low water. Fertilize after blooming.

LIRIOPE
Liriope platyphylla
10 inches tall
Zone 6
Purple flowers, mid- to late summer; dark green or green-and-white, strap-shaped leaves; slightly acidic soil; full sun/part shade; low water. Tolerates drought.

MAIDEN PINK
Dianthus deltoides
1 foot tall
Zone 3
Rose or red flowers, spring to fall; narrow, green or blue-green leaves; well-drained, near-neutral soil; full sun; low water. Fertilize twice during summer.

Designing to Conceal

Every yard has objects or views that would be better unseen. The projects in this section show how you can use design techniques to reduce or hide undesirable views, call attention to desirable ones, and flatter the best features of your house and yard.

When landscaping to conceal certain features or views, the challenge is to hide problems without having your improvements call attention to the problem itself. To accomplish this trick, use the design principle known as repetition. For example, if you use a fence or hedge to conceal a piece of machinery and that is the only hedge or fence in your yard, it tends to draw attention to itself. However, if you repeat the same hedge or fence in other parts of your yard, the features you are trying to conceal will blend into the overall design.

Other projects in this section show you how to use specially designed beds to draw attention away from a foundation that is too high or too low. You will also learn how to use arbors or trees to frame views that lack depth or interest, as well as techniques for concealing unattractive views in your landscape. In these situations, designing to conceal is often a simple matter of using plants and structures to balance horizontal or vertical lines that are a little too strong. ❧

Creating a New View

Frame desired features, conceal unwanted ones, or simply add a beautiful element to your landscape by installing an arbor such as the one shown here, or by planting a border of evergreens or native plants that grow vigorously in your area. There are virtually hundreds of ways to enhance the best features of your landscape, screen less pleasant views, and add value to your property.

Arbors are traditional architectural features that support climbing plants and add vertical accents. Your arbor can act as a beautiful gateway to a garden path, separate one area of your landscape from another, and allow you to frame a view in the most attractive way possible. Most home and garden centers carry prefabricated arbors that can be set in place quickly.

Screening and defining a view can also be accomplished with plants alone. The classic evergreen hedge is a handsome, year-round feature that can screen unattractive features and define your landscape. Many juniper and arborvitae species are well suited to this task.

For a less formal approach, native plant species will provide variation and natural good looks, as well as attract birds and butterflies to your garden. ❧

INSTALLING AN ARBOR

If the arbor you choose is made of wood, a treatment with wood preservative or a good coat of paint will add years to its life.

When you prepare the holes in which your arbor will be set, take note of the length of its legs to be certain it will stand at the appropriate height.

Match climbing plants to your arbor's strength and consider the conditions they need for growth. Plant 8 to 12 inches from outside of arbor to allow maintenance without disturbing plants. ❦

HAVE ON HAND:

- ▶ Prefabricated arbor
- ▶ Four marking stakes
- ▶ Hammer
- ▶ Posthole digger
- ▶ Five gallons of gravel
- ▶ Carpenter's level
- ▶ Tape measure
- ▶ Topsoil

Optional
- ▶ Mulch

Place arbor in your chosen location. Check its position from both sides for the best aesthetics. Mark position of each leg with a stake.

Use a post-hole digger to make 1-foot-deep holes where stakes are placed. Reserve soil for use in Step 7.

Pour a bed of gravel in each hole that the arbor legs will rest on. Add gravel so that arbor stands straight and at the height you want.

Place arbor legs in holes and fill around them with gravel. Use a carpenter's level to check that the structure is plumb and level.

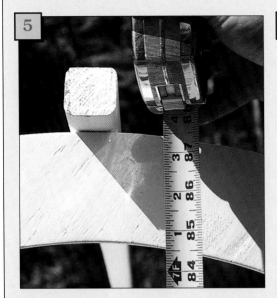

Measure clearance height through the arbor. The height should be at least 7 feet. Make necessary adjustments, recheck plumb, and level.

Fill each hole with remaining gravel to within 2 inches of the soil surface, making certain that arbor stays in place and is level.

For a better appearance, use soil from Step 2 to finish filling each hole; tamp down firmly. Use mulch or other material under arbor if you wish.

Plant a climbing vine 8 to 12 inches outside each arbor leg. Water thoroughly and mulch. Train vines to arbor as they grow.

HERE'S HOW

PLANTS FOR ARBORS

Your standing arbor will be an invitation to grow flowering vines that will curl around and cascade over it, enhancing the effect of your arbor.

Use such annuals as morning glory or hyacinth bean for fast, seasonal cover. For a more permanent effect try clematis. The hybrid Jackmanii, for example, offers mid-season, purple bloom. Avoid plants with thorns—climbing roses can snag clothing and scratch the skin.

Alternatives

AN EVERGREEN BORDER

Evergreens in an easily created border or hedge can work wonderfully either to conceal or to frame any spot in your landscape. A single-species border will function as if it were a uniform and solid hedge. A border made of mixed species or varieties of plants will have a less formal feeling and create an interesting view from a distance. For tight spots, a single-species hedge is most effective.

When choosing your plants, consider the ultimate size you want your border to be. Junipers, arborvitae, boxwoods, and yews all make excellent choices for a border that can be maintained at or will grow less than 12 feet high.

Where a taller screen is desired, you can use pine, blue spruce, Norway spruce, taller hemlocks, or arborvitaes and yews left untrimmed. Check with your local garden center for plant recommendations for your specific area. Ensure your success by using plants that will do well in your design. Single specimens of large evergreen trees such as hemlocks or pines work well for framing attractive views or for screening out undesirable ones. 🌸

A LOCALLY ADAPTED SCREEN

Plants indigenous to your region, or to another part of the world with a similar climate, make the sturdiest and most reliable screen of all. Perfectly adapted to their climate and environment, they can withstand fluctuations in temperature and moisture that other species cannot. For example, lavender and rosemary, two plants originally from the Mediterranean region, both thrive in the similar climate of California, as shown here. The use of locally adapted plants will enhance your feeling of harmony with the surrounding landscape.

Because native plants grow best in their "home zones," make sure the ones you choose are native to your local climate. Visit area nature trails and arboretums to get acquainted with pretty native plants, particularly those that might provide food and habitat for birds or other wildlife while framing or screening special views.

As native plants have become more popular in home landscapes, it has become easier to buy nursery-grown specimens. It is illegal to dig many native species, so always buy your plants from a reputable nursery or from a catalog specializing in nursery-grown native plants. 🌸

Concealing A/C and Pool Machinery

There is nothing attractive about the appearance of heat pumps, air conditioners, propane gas tanks, swimming pool pumps, or other machinery. You can conceal them by building or planting a screen that blends with the rest of your landscape. To make sure that the screen does not interfere with the operation of machinery, allow at least 2 feet of clearance all around and pay close attention to the location of buried utility lines. With heat pumps and air conditioners, you will also need to plan for the drainage of the condensation they produce.

You can create a screen by using lattice panels, shrubs, fencing, or a combination of these materials. Blend the screen into your landscape by making it match or coordinate with other structures. For example, you might paint a lattice panel to complement your house's siding or trim. Or, you could use a section of wood fence that matches other fencing used in your yard. Arrange outdoor seating so it faces away from the screened machinery. Also, locate ornamental features, such as a water garden or attractive statuary, where they will draw attention away from less attractive objects. ❧

INSTALLING A TRELLIS

A framed trellis will let air circulate freely around your machinery. This 4-foot-wide panel stands 4 ½ feet high, but you can make it any size you like. ❧

HAVE ON HAND:

- ▶ Tape measure
- ▶ Two wood stakes
- ▶ Hammer
- ▶ String
- ▶ Carpenter's level
- ▶ Posthole digger
- ▶ Shovel
- ▶ Two 6-foot-long 2 x 4s (posts)
- ▶ Pencil
- ▶ Saw
- ▶ Lattice panel 4 x 4 feet
- ▶ Box of ½-inch galvanized nails
- ▶ Four 45-inch-long 1 x 2 fir strips
- ▶ Two 4-foot-long 1 x 2 fir strips
- ▶ Fine-grade sandpaper
- ▶ Damp rag
- ▶ Exterior paint
- ▶ Paintbrush

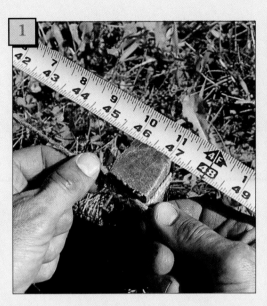

Drive stakes 46 inches apart where posts will be located. Tie string between stakes. Use level to make sure it is straight.

Dig post holes 18 inches deep. Set posts in holes and refill halfway. Check with level again to make sure posts are straight. Firm soil.

Mark posts 54 inches from ground. Run a string between marks and adjust to make it level. Mark string line on posts with pencil.

Fill holes, checking again to make sure posts are straight and tops are level. If top of the post projects above 54-inch mark, trim it to length.

Nail 45-inch-long fir strips to outside edges of lattice panel at top and bottom, leaving a 1 ½-inch margin on each side. Repeat on back.

Nail top corners of lattice panel to top fronts of posts. Check to make sure panel is horizontally level. Nail panel bottom to posts.

Nail fir strips to lattice panel sides and posts, spacing nails 8 inches apart. Sand lightly to remove splinters.

Clean panel with damp rag. When dry, paint the panel and posts or finish with sealant, stain, or polyurethane varnish.

HERE'S HOW

CUTTING LATTICE PANELS

Lattice panels are usually sold in 4 x 8-foot pieces. Because they are so large and flimsy, the panels can be difficult to cut by yourself. Some stores will cut the lattice panels for you, provided you buy the whole panel. If cutting a lattice panel at home, get two helpers to support the ends of the panel as you cut. When working by yourself, try placing long pieces of scrap lumber under the panels to support them while you saw.

Alternatives

HEDGE

If you already have a foundation planting close to machinery or anything else you want to hide, an easy solution is to extend the planting that already exists. In the photograph on the left, a possibly unattractive house foundation is concealed by arborvitae. This foundation planting of small evergreens can easily be extended as a hedge, and arborvitae is a good choice as it provides year-round concealment and can be kept to desirable height by clipping. Plants for screening purposes should not be so tall that they block more attractive views. Upright hedges require less space than mixed plantings, which explains their popularity in small, cottage-type gardens.

If a pathway or open area lies between your existing plants and, for instance, machinery, you can still use this approach and have the result look natural by making the area in front of the machinery into a planting bed. The key is to plant the screening bed with evergreens or shrubs that are used in other parts of your yard so that it looks like a part of your overall design. If nearby areas of your yard include a formal, clipped hedge, you can continue that element as your screen. ❧

FENCING

You can instantly hide machinery from view by erecting a fence. As with other types of concealing screens, you can avoid calling attention to the fence by using the kind that appears in other parts of your yard, or by matching the fence to nearby colors and textures. For example, if the machinery is located near a wood deck, natural wood fencing that mimics the style of the deck would work well. Near swimming pools where there are concrete surfaces, a low fence or wall made of perforated concrete might make an attractive screen.

Where fences are not already present in the landscape, you can still use a panel of fence to hide unattractive machinery if you keep the fence low and plant shrubs in front of it to make the fence less noticeable. Vertical slat fences, made from narrow boards nailed to top and bottom rails, are especially useful since their strong vertical lines draw the eye up and away from the fence. In addition, if you wish to make an attractive and useful enclosure in a small yard, add fencing at a right angle to the fence that is meant to conceal. ❧

Screening a High Foundation

THIS GARDEN THRIVES WITH

SUN

WATER

SOIL

Full sun to part shade   **Medium**   **Average to acidic**

Plants grown around the foundation of your house help frame the building by nestling it into the site. If the distance between the bottom of your windows and the ground is more than 4 feet, foundation shrubs will meld the house and grounds together gracefully while hiding less attractive features such as weep holes, crawlspace vents, and concrete block masonry.

Place the tallest plants at the back of your foundation bed. They need not be heavy bloomers, for an important part of their job is to serve as a backdrop for more colorful plants in the foreground. Include some evergreens to keep your foundation screened year round. Variations in form and texture among foundation shrubs add interest, but repeating the same combination of shrubs on both sides of the front door helps maintain a sense of unity within the landscape.

When fully grown, foundation shrubs should not crowd windows. Shop carefully for cultivars that will grow to appropriate heights and widths for the places where they will be planted. Also, plan for water runoff from gutters and downspouts. If you have drainage problems, install perforated drainage pipes under plantings as you prepare the soil.

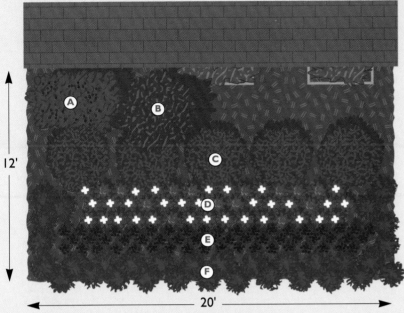

12'

20'

1. Dig the soil 14 inches deep for the foundation bed. Remove debris. Work in a 4- to 6-inch layer of soil amendments, including equal parts compost, peat moss, and composted manure. Don't cultivate the soil within 15 inches of your house. Mulch over this strip with shredded bark or pine needles.

2. Dig planting hole for photinia (A) 3 feet from corner end of the house. Set plant in hole, spread out roots, and check planting depth so that the highest roots will be covered with 1 inch of soil. Refill hole halfway, flood with water, and finish filling hole with soil.

3. Plant azalea (B) the same way, but set it higher in the planting hole. As you refill the hole, layer in 2 inches of soil, then 1 inch of peat moss. Flood the hole with water. Repeat layers until the top roots barely show through soil.

4. Plant boxwoods (C) the same as photinia, 6 feet from the house. Make sure they are upright and evenly spaced.

5. Excavate tulip bed 1 foot deep. Mix bone meal or high phosphorous bulb fertilizer into the bottom of the bed, following manufacturer's instructions. Set tulip bulbs (D) in a three-tiered arrangement as shown, with pointed ends of the bulbs facing up. If you are using two colors of tulips, mix the two colors in all three tiers, with a few more of the darker-colored tulips in the back tier and the lighter-colored ones in the front tier.

6. Rake soil smooth in remainder of bed, and set forget-me-nots (E) in an offset, three-tiered arrangement, as shown. Mulch all plants with a 2-inch layer of shredded bark.

7. Set English ivy (F) in foreground of bed, cultivating the soil slightly if it became compacted when you installed the larger plants. Mulch lightly and water well.

PLANT LIST

A. Chinese photinia, 1, 10 to 30 feet tall

B. Azalea, 1, 10 feet tall

C. Dwarf boxwood, 5, 4 feet tall

D. Darwin tulip, 45, 24 to 30 inches tall

E. Forget-me-not, 55, 8 inches tall

F. English ivy, 32, 8 inches tall

(See next page for more on plants.)

HERE'S HOW

WINDOW BOXES

Window boxes with colorful annuals such as pansies can be enjoyed from inside and outside your house. Allow a 1-inch recess between the top of the box and the soil line to keep the soil from splattering. To replenish, replace the soil every year and periodically water with liquid fertilizer.

Plants for a High Foundation

You can install the plants in this design all at once or establish them in stages. The shrubs and English ivy can be planted in the spring or fall, or even during the summer if you give them plenty of water. Tulips should be planted in the fall. Since they bloom only in the spring, you may want to set a trio of chrysanthemums in the same part of the planting bed. Chrysanthemums grow during the summer while tulips are becoming dormant and bloom in the fall when tulips have disappeared, so the two plants make great partners.

The forget-me-nots may grow as perennials or biennials, depending on your climate. They often die back in late summer, and their new growth appears in the fall. Learn to recognize their leaves so you don't accidentally pull them out during routine weeding. ❧

CHINESE PHOTINIA
Photinia serrulata
10-30 feet tall
Zone 6
White flower clusters, spring; red berries; stiff, dark green leaves to 8 inches; acid soil; needs morning sun to discourage mildew; medium water. New growth copper, turning reddish in winter.

AZALEA
Rhododendron hybrids
2-10 feet tall
Zone 3
Pink, white, red, orange, or yellow flowers, spring; small, leathery leaves through winter on evergreen cultivars; acid soil essential; sun/part shade; medium water. Wide range of cold/heat tolerance.

DWARF BOXWOOD
Buxus sempervirens 'Suffructicosa'
4 feet tall
Zone 5
Flowers insignificant; small, glossy, dark green leaves on thickly layered woody branches, dense, mounded foliage; acid soil; sun/part shade; medium water.

DARWIN TULIP
Tulipa hybrids
24-30 inches tall
Zone 3
Red, white, or yellow flowers on sturdy stems, spring; some variegated leaves; any soil; sun/part shade; medium water. Plant 8 inches deep for best bloom after first year.

FORGET-ME-NOT
Myosotis alpestris
8 inches tall
Zone 3
Tiny, abundant blue flowers, spring; small, dainty leaves form green mounds; slightly acidic soil; partial shade; medium water. Very hard. Reseeds for perennial effect.

ENGLISH IVY
Hedera helix
8 inches tall
Zone 5
No flowers when grown as ground cover; leaves dark, glossy, classic ivy shape on woody stems; dry soil; deep shade. Grows in shaded areas where other plants fail.

CARE FOR YOUR FOUNDATION PLANTING

SPRING Lightly prune photinia if needed. Remove weeds. Prune back English ivy runners. Keep rhododendron soil acid with an acidifying fertilizer, and fertilize each shrub with ¼ cup of 10-10-10 fertilizer. Plant pansies or other flowers in window boxes.

SUMMER After flowers fade, lightly prune photinia to shape. Use hedge trimmers to keep boxwoods uniform in size and shape. Allow tulip foliage to die back naturally. Lightly fertilize tulips and forget-me-nots with a high phosphorous fertilizer.

FALL Rake up any leaves that have fallen from nearby trees. Pull all the weeds and renew the mulches around shrubs with fresh material. Replace tulip bulbs if they did not flower well in the spring. Clean out window boxes. ❧

Alternative

EVERGREEN SHRUBS

Shrubs that hold their foliage all year are the hardest-working plants in your foundation beds. Evergreens not only screen the house foundation, they also frame the house in winter with bright splashes of green. Evergreens such as junipers often serve as homes for winter birds, and shrubs that produce berries supplement wildlife winter diets.

Evergreens are generally divided into broad- and narrow-leaved types. The ones with broad leaves, such as euonymous and Japanese holly, sometimes drop their leaves if winter weather becomes unusually harsh and then leaf out anew in the spring. Most evergreens with narrow leaves are conifers. They usually have a piney scent and grow to clearly defined shapes, such as upright pyramids and columns. Others are dwarf, with a low, wide growth habit.

While all evergreens make wonderful backdrops for more colorful plants, there are many varieties that are noticeable for their color as well. The branches of narrow-leaved junipers may be tipped in gold, and some cultivars become blue-green or purple in winter. Many euonymus cultivars have richly variegated leaves. 🌿

JAPANESE HOLLY
Ilex crenata
4-15 feet tall
Zone 5
Greenish-white flowers, late spring; black berries in fall; foliage deep green, glossy, with small leaves similar to boxwoods; slightly acid soil; sun/part shade; medium water.

EUONYMUS
Euonymus fortunei **'Emerald Gaiety'**
4 feet tall
Zone 5
Flowers insignificant; variegated, green and yellowish-white foliage on woody stems; acid soil; sun; medium water. Forms an erect mound or may be shaped by pruning.

JUNIPER
Juniperus chinensis
4-20 feet tall
Zone 4
Flowers insignificant; narrow, stiff needles on woody, spreading branches; acid soil; sun/part shade; medium water. Foliage color green, blue-green, or gold-tipped, depending on cultivar. Blue berries, as shown, or black in some cultivars. Shapes and heights vary.

DWARF JAPANESE RED BARBERRY
Berberis thunbergii **'Crimson Pygmy'**
2-3 feet tall
Zone 5
Small yellow flowers, spring, followed by berries; reddish-purple foliage turns bright red in fall; acid soil; sun/part shade; medium water. Responds well to pruning.

JAPANESE YEW
Taxus cuspidata
4-20 feet tall
Zone 4
Flowers insignificant; needles dense, dark green; branches spread to form curtain; acid soil; sun/part shade; medium water. Pyramid shape most common; cultivars vary in height, shape, and regional adaptation. Fruit is poisonous and must not be eaten.

Masking a Low Foundation

THIS GARDEN THRIVES WITH

SUN
Full sun to shade

WATER
Medium

SOIL
Average

If your home sits very low to the ground, you can make it seem taller by layering plants into foundation beds that gently slope away from the house. Crowding the foundation beds with massive shrubs would make the house look smaller. A spreading bed that skirts the foundation has the opposite effect. It pulls the frame forward, so the house appears tall and airy.

For the health of your house and your plants, the first step is to grade the site so that the house sits a few inches higher than the adjoining parts of your yard. Houses where the ground has not been graded away from the house may suffer water damage to sills or siding. Make necessary repairs before you begin any landscaping project. You can hire a landscape contractor to grade the site or do it yourself with a spade, rake, and a truckload of good topsoil.

Since small houses all too easily appear cluttered, try to keep your design lines simple and use walkways and edgings to create a neat and spacious look. Choosing light colors for your house and flowers will make each element appear larger. Using bright colors as accents will add interest to your flower beds as they conceal your foundation. ❧

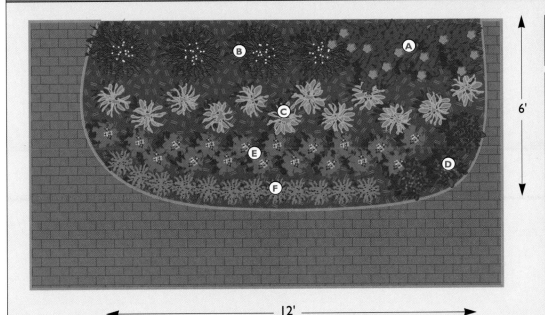

6'

12'

PLANT LIST

A. Trumpet vine, 1, 30 feet tall

B. Shasta daisy, 4, 3 feet tall

C. Artemisia, 12, 3 feet tall

D. Butterfly flower, 3, 18 inches tall

E. Pansy, 18, 9 inches tall

F. Bugleweed, 12, 6 inches tall

(See next page for more on plants.)

1. Amend the soil in your new bed by digging in a 3-inch layer of humus, such as a mixture of compost and peat moss, and two cups of 10-10-10 or other balanced fertilizer. Unless your soil is sandy, also mix in 50 pounds of sand to help the soil drain well.

2. Rake cultivated soil so that the part of the bed 2 feet closest to the house is 3 inches higher than the rest of the bed. Pave walkway with bricks or stones (see Installing a Garden Walkway, page 30).

3. Plant the trumpet vine (A) 15 inches from the house. Drive a 6-foot wooden stake into the ground midway between the house and the base of the vine. Tie the vine to the stake with cotton twine.

4. Standing on a board placed in the middle of the bed, plant the shasta daisies (B) 2 feet apart at the back of the bed. Remove the board.

5. Plant artemisias (C) 2 feet apart, offset as shown, in front of the shasta daisies. Plant pansies (E) spaced 1 foot apart, and also offset, in front of the artemisias.

6. Plant a group of butterfly flowers (D) 2 feet apart in a curve on the right. Plant an edging of bugleweed (F) at front 6 inches apart.

7. Water the entire bed and mulch between plants with a layer of shredded bark.

HERE'S HOW

ANNUAL VINES

You can use an annual vine as a vertical accent for a low foundation bed, and train it up a simple string, wire, or wooden trellis attached to stakes in the ground. Try climbing nasturtium, morning glory, scarlet runner beans for bright red blooms, or hyacinth bean for a touch of purple.

Plants for a Low Foundation

With the trumpet vine as a vertical accent, this simple arrangement of easy-care flowers revolves around the artemisias. Their neutral color and soft texture prevent possible clashes among nearby plants, while melding the house and the flower bed together visually. The bugleweed edging gives the bed a finished look while balancing the bright hues of the butterfly flowers.

Layering the plants so that the tallest ones are in the rear of the bed and the smallest ones in the front creates a feeling of depth that masks the low foundation while allowing sunlight to reach all of the flowers.

Keep this in mind when trying different annuals as accent plants in the bed. In warm climates where pansies fade in early summer, bright yellow portulacas or dwarf yellow marigolds will extend the flowering season. 🌾

TRUMPET VINE
Campsis radicans
30 feet tall
Zone 4
Orange flowers, summer through fall; green leaves drop off in fall; any acidic soil; sun/shade; medium water. Clings to support with aerial rootlets.

SHASTA DAISY
Leucanthemum maximum (formerly Chrysanthemum x superbum)
3 foot tall
Zone 5
White daisies, spring and early summer; dark green foliage forms rosettes that persist through winter; rich, moist soil; sun/light shade; medium water.

ARTEMISIA
Artemisia ludoviciana 'Silver King'
3 feet tall
Zone 5
Tiny, grayish-white flowers, summer; silver gray foliage, fragrant if crushed; any well-drained soil; full sun/light afternoon shade; low water.

BUTTERFLY FLOWER
Schizanthus pinnatus
18 inches tall
All zones
Pink, purple, white, or yellow flowers, summer to fall; feathery foliage; neutral soil; sun in cool weather/part shade in summer; medium water.

PANSY
Viola x wittrockiana
9 inches tall
All zones
Flowers in many colors with or without blotches or "faces"; glossy green leaves; rich, fertile soil; full sun/part shade; medium water.

BUGLEWEED
Ajuga reptans
6 inches tall
Zone 3
Blue flower spikes, early summer; reddish-green leaves form rosettes; any well-drained soil; full sun/dark shade; medium water.

CARE FOR YOUR LOW FOUNDATION BED

SPRING Prune trumpet vine to stimulate new growth and heavy flowering. Install support as needed for new vine growth. Remove weeds, renew mulches, and set out pansies. Add butterfly flowers after last frost has passed.

SUMMER Trim faded flowers from shasta daisies to encourage repeat blooms. Pinch tops from artemisias to promote compact, bushy growth. After bugleweed blooms, trim off flower spikes. In hot summer areas, pull up pansies.

FALL Pot up your healthiest butterfly flower and bring it indoors as a winter houseplant. Cut rooted basal stems from shasta daisies and replant them. Dig bugleweed from awkward places and replant. Set out new pansies. 🌾

Alternative

USING NEUTRALS AND BRIGHT COLORS

The key design elements of this flower bed can be fine-tuned to match your house and site. You will always want to use light, neutral colors to unify the bed with your house and to include an edging for a crisp, maintained look. However, the vine might be a clematis or wisteria, or you could opt for a columnar evergreen shrub as a vertical accent.

In cold climates, where gray-leaved foliage plants have trouble surviving winter, you can use annual bedding plants, such as dusty miller or annual baby's-breath, as your neutral plants. Or use white flowers in place of the neutrals. For example, a central drift of white snapdragons will lighten up a low foundation and help to harmonize the colors of more vibrant plants.

With suitable neutral plants in place, you can have fun trying different annuals for splashes of summer color and interesting variations in form and texture. Choose small annuals that are properly scaled to the size of the bed, such as verbenas, dianthus, marigolds, or dwarf petunias. Tiny annuals like lobelia, ageratum, or sweet alyssum could be used as edging plants. ✤

SILVER SANTOLINA
Santolina chamaecyparissus
18-24 inches tall
Zone 6
Little, yellow, button-like flowers, summer, if plants not clipped; small, stiff, silver-gray leaves with cottony texture; any well-drained soil; full sun; low water.

LAMB'S EARS
Stachys byzantina
12-18 inches tall
Zone 4
Small, purple flowers attractive to bees, mid-summer; gray-green leaves have texture of fur; moist, slightly acidic soil; sun/part shade; medium water.

DAYLILY
Hemerocallis hybrid **'Stella de Oro'**
11 inches tall
Zone 3
Bright yellow flowers with green throats, spring through summer; long, strap-like. green leaves; moist, fertile soil; strongest in full sun; occasional water during dry spells.

CLEMATIS
Clematis x Jackmanii
20 feet long
Zone 3
Large, purple flowers on new wood, summer; glossy, green leaves; rich, neutral soil; full sun/afternoon shade; medium water. Clings by curving stems around support.

EVERGREEN CANDYTUFT
Iberis sempervirens
10 inches tall
Zone 4
Clusters of white flowers, spring; dark green leaves persist in winter; any well-drained soil; sun/part shade; medium water. Cut back after flowering for repeat blooms.

Hiding Utility Boxes and Wellheads

THIS GARDEN THRIVES WITH

SUN	WATER	SOIL
Full sun to part shade	Medium	Average

Utility equipment such as gas meters, wellheads, and electrical switch boxes are functional but unattractive landscape features. Their job is to keep your house comfortable, and it's up to you to make these awkward objects blend into your home landscape.

Several practical matters must be considered when concealing utility equipment. Digging near buried pipes or wires can have disastrous results, so find out where these lines are before beginning this project. If you do not know the location of underground lines, ask your local utility companies for this information. If utility equipment is located in a defined easement, which means the space is under the legal control of the utility companies, it's wise to limit your investment in any landscaping projects there.

In many cases, utility equipment can be camouflaged quickly and inexpensively by painting it a dark color and surrounding it with plants. Or, build a simple wooden box, paint it dark green, and place it over the equipment. When concealing gas or water meters with a box, include a hinged door so that repair people and meter-readers have easy access. And be sure any shutoff valves remain within easy reach. 🌸

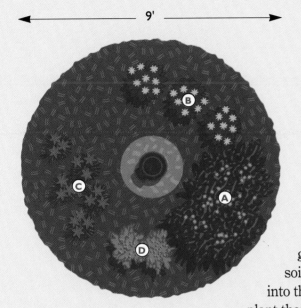

9'

PLANT LIST

A. Lilac, 1, to 20 feet tall

B. Chrysanthemum, 3, 2 feet tall

C. Asiatic hybrid lily, 5, 3 feet tall

D. Dwarf astilbe, 2, 1 foot tall

(See next page for more on plants.)

2. Select the side of the wellhead with the easiest access. Leave this side open. Opposite the open side and 3 feet from the wellhead, plant one lilac (A) at the same depth it grew in its container. If soil is acidic, mix ½ cup lime into the planting hole. Water plant thoroughly.

3. Plant chrysanthemums (B) 2 feet from the wellhead, barely covering the roots with soil. Water and mulch. On the opposite side of the wellhead, plant five lily bulbs (C) in a clump, allowing 10 inches between bulbs. Cover lily bulbs with 4 inches of soil. Plant astilbes (D) 1 foot from the lilies.

1. If your wellhead has not been serviced recently, consider having it inspected before completing this project. If the wellhead is in good working order, proceed to clean and paint it, if needed. Dark green or brown are the best colors for outdoor camouflage. Finally, mulch around the wellhead with pebbles, bark, or another clean material. Spread the mulch in a 1-foot-wide collar around the wellhead.

4. Water all plants thoroughly, and spread 2 inches of organic mulch such as shredded bark beneath lilac and chrysanthemums. Mulch lilies and astilbes after they show vigorous new growth.

HERE'S HOW

WIRE BASKETS FOR BULBS

In many areas rodents are likely to dine on lily bulbs. To prevent rodent damage, loosely wrap individual lily bulbs in baskets made of ½-inch wire mesh before you plant them. Leave the top open, but have the chicken wire extend at least 2 inches above the bulb top.

Plants to Hide a Wellhead

Although lilacs can eventually grow to 20 feet, they grow very slowly and remain small for several years. Meanwhile, the astilbes benefit from the shelter of the lilac, and more short-lived, colorful plants bring lively contrast in texture and form to the planting. The upright form of the lilies is especially effective for camouflaging the wellhead. Lilies can be picky about the places where they are grown, but the hybrid Asiatic types are easy to please with good drainage and full sun.

Chrysanthemums form a mound of dark green foliage during most of the summer, and then bloom heavily in early fall. Many cultivars are dependable, hardy perennials to Zone 5. In colder climates, you can use potted mums for quick summer color. 🌸

ASIATIC HYBRID LILY
Lilium hybrids
3 feet tall
Zone 4
Flowers in shades of red and yellow, summer; dark green leaves on upright stalks; very well-drained soil; full sun; medium water.

CHRYSANTHEMUM
Chrysanthemum morifolium 'Bristol Gold'
2 feet tall
Zone 5
Gold flowers late summer to fall; green foliage; average soil; full sun; medium water. Fertilize early summer.

ASTILBE
Astilbe chinensis 'Pumila'
1 foot tall
Zone 4
Pink flowers, late summer; ferny foliage; average soil; full sun/part shade; medium water. A dwarf that forms low ground cover.

LILAC
Syringa vulgaris
to 20 feet tall
Zone 3
Fragrant lilac, pink, or white flowers, spring; glossy green leaves; moist, neutral soil; full sun; medium water. Mulching is desirable.

CARE FOR YOUR WELLHEAD PLANTING

SPRING Renew mulch beneath lilac. To encourage new branches, pinch back mums when stems are 6 inches tall. Fertilize lilies, mums, and astilbes with light application of balanced fertilizer.

SUMMER Pull weeds as needed to keep planting neat. Stake lilies with thin wood or bamboo stakes painted green. Pinch back growing tips of mums a second time in early summer. Deadhead astilbes.

FALL Cut back lily stalks at the ground just before first hard frost. After the ground freezes, mulch lilies and astilbes with evergreen boughs. 🌸

Alternative

SCREENING SHRUBS FOR UTILITY BOXES

One of the simplest ways to screen utility boxes from view is to flank them with low shrubs. In very cold climates, your choice of planting material is limited to dwarf junipers and pruned-to-height arborvitae, but from Zone 5 southward numerous small shrubs are available in a wide range of leaf types and growth habits.

Since you don't want to call attention to the object you are trying to hide, choose shrubs that are attractive yet common. Concealing utility boxes is yet another place in your landscape where the design principle known as repetition will help fool the eye. When you decide upon a small shrub or shrub grouping to use in screening utility equipment, use the same plant or plants in other areas of your landscape. This approach is especially important if you choose shrubs with reddish foliage or shrubs with showy flowers.

The shrubs listed below require little care beyond occasional pruning and fertilization. In addition to these, you will find more plants useful for screening on the following two pages. Remember to steer clear of buried utility lines when planting shrubs or other screening plants around utility boxes, and always allow easy access for equipment maintenance and repair. 🌿

WEIGELA
Weigela 'Florida'
3 feet tall
Zone 4
Pink flowers late spring; green or variegated foliage; well-drained soil; full sun; medium water. Prune lightly when flowers fade. Apply mulch in winter.

YAUPON HOLLY
Ilex vomitoria
to 5 feet tall
Zone 7
Flowers insignificant; tiny green leaves on stiff, woody stems; any soil; full sun; medium water. Female plants produce berries if pollinated.

FRASER'S PHOTINIA
Photinia x fraseri
4 feet tall
Zone 6
White flowers, summer; pointed green leaves red when young; berries in fall; any soil; full/ part sun; medium water.

DWARF HEAVENLY BAMBOO
Nandina domestica
1-4 feet tall
Zone 6
White flowers, early summer; glossy green leaves and berries turn red in winter; moist soil; full sun/part shade; medium water.

HYDRANGEA
Hydrangea macrophylla
4 feet tall
Zone 6
Blue or pink flowers, mid- to late summer; large green leaves; slightly acidic soil enriched with organic matter; full sun to part shade; regular water.

A Guide to Fast-Growing Plants for Screening

SHRUBS

Shrubs require little maintenance and can be chosen to provide year-round beauty. They also provide food and habitat for birds and butterflies.

FORSYTHIA
Forsythia x intermedia
10 feet tall
Zone 5
Yellow flowers, early spring; green leaves, arching stems; well-drained soil; sun/part shade; medium water. Fertilize in spring. Prune before summer.

GLOSSY ABELIA
Abelia x grandiflora
6 feet tall
Zone 6
Pinkish-white flowers midsummer to fall; reddish-green or variegated leaves, evergreen in warm climates; well-drained soil; full sun/part shade; medium water.

TREES

Let low limbs sweep the ground for maximum effect when using trees for screening. Avoid injuring the tree trunks with mowers and other equipment.

WHITE PINE
Pinus strobus
60 feet tall
Zone 2
Insignificant flowers; evergreen needles on spreading branches; slightly acidic soil; full sun/part shade; medium water while young.

AMUR MAPLE
Acer ginnala
10 feet tall
Zone 2
Yellowish flowers, spring; deciduous, green leaves turn yellow or red in fall; any good soil; full sun; medium water while young.

VINES

Use hardy perennial vines to cover fences where they can screen out the view beyond, or put them to work as ground covers on slopes.

HARDY KIWI
Actinidia arguta
to 30 feet tall
Zone 4
Insignificant flowers; lustrous leaves; small edible fruits in fall; rich soil; full sun; medium water. Tie to supports. Prune in winter.

FIVELEAF AKEBIA
Akebia quinata
to 30 feet tall
Zone 4
Purple flowers, spring; evergreen in mild climates; well-drained soil; full sun/part shade; medium water.

ORNAMENTAL GRASSES

Mass ornamental grasses or plant them in large clumps for good screening. Grasses are accentuated in the wind; dried foliage adds winter interest.

SILVER GRASS
Miscanthus sinensis
6 feet tall
Zone 5
Airy, silvery plumes, late summer into winter; long green leaves; average soil; full sun; medium water.

FEATHER REED GRASS
Calamagrostis acutiflora
6 feet tall
Zone 5
Bluish panicles, early summer, tan in fall; reedy, green leaves; average soil; full sun; medium water.

JAPANESE BARBERRY
Berberis thunbergii
5 feet tall
Zone 5
Flowers insignificant; some variegated leaves; prickly stems; red berries in fall; average soil; full sun/part shade; low water once established.

CRAPE MYRTLE
Lagerstroemia indica
3-25 feet tall
Zone 7
Red, pink, white, or lavender flowers, midsummer; dark green leaves, peeling bark; rich, well-drained soil; full sun; medium water. Prune in winter.

OREGON GRAPE
Mahonia aquifolium
3-6 feet tall
Zone 5
Yellow flowers, spring; spiny leaves green in summer, red in winter; purple fruits, late summer; moist, acidic soil; part shade; medium water.

EUROPEAN BEECH
Fagus sylvatica
50 feet tall
Zone 5
Flowers insignificant; deciduous, reddish-green leaves, low spreading branches; slightly acidic soil; full sun, medium water.

SMOKE TREE
Cotinus coggygria
to 25 feet tall
Zone 5
Purple flower stalks spring into summer, small flowers drop quickly; reddish leaves turn bright red or yellow in fall; any soil; full sun; medium water when young.

GOLDEN-RAIN TREE
Koelreuteria paniculata
30 feet tall
Zone 5
Yellow flower clusters, summer, followed by seed pods; green leaves yellow in fall; any good soil; full sun; medium water.

JAPANESE WISTERIA
Wisteria floribunda
to 40 feet tall
Zone 4
Fragrant purple or pink flowers, spring; green foliage; acidic soil, no lime or fertilizer; full/filtered sun; medium water. Prune in winter.

CAROLINA JESSAMINE
Gelsemium sempervirens
to 20 feet tall
Zone 7
Yellow, trumpet-like flowers, early spring; dark evergreen foliage; any soil; full sun/part shade; medium water. Prune annually after third year.

GOLDEN CLEMATIS
Clematis tangutica
to 15 feet tall
Zone 4
Yellow, bell-shaped flowers, early summer; deciduous, green leaves; near-neutral soil; full sun/part shade; medium water. Prune to size.

FOUNTAIN GRASS
Pennisetum incomptum
4 feet tall
Zone 6
Bristly, reddish-beige panicles, midsummer to fall; thin, green leaves; average soil; full sun/part shade; medium water.

BLUE OAT GRASS
Helictotrichon sempervirens
2 feet tall
Zone 4
Oat-like flower stalks, late spring; blue-green leaves in tight clumps; any well-drained soil; full sun; medium water. Trim in late summer.

RAVENNA GRASS
Erianthus ravennae
9 feet tall
Zone 6
Silvery, purple panicles, late summer, persist into winter; silvery, green leaves; well-drained soil; full sun; medium water.

Enhancing Difficult Terrain

Some of the most challenging places in your landscape can become its most dramatic features. Sweeping slopes, gnarled tree roots that lie at the soil's surface, and areas that receive heavy shade all have great potential. But rather than trying to change their nature, it's best to meet problem sites on their own terms. Before you decide on changes, let yourself imagine what the site might look like if nature had a century to work its wonders. Perhaps an eroded slope created by bulldozers would turn into a craggy stone outcropping. Maybe a dark, shady spot would become a moss-covered glen. The best way to landscape difficult spots is to mimic and accelerate the ecological changes that would occur naturally over time.

Difficult sites often hold hidden surprises underground, so spend time studying your problem area before you begin an improvement project. If you suspect that solid rock lies beneath a thin layer of soil, pound a thin metal rod into the ground to check the soil's depth. This is also a good way to find suitable planting pockets among large tree roots. As you make plans for enhancing your difficult site, eliminate natural hazards by filling in sunken holes or sawing off dead tree limbs. It's easier to see the potential in a problem area after it has been cleaned up and made safe. 🌸

Transforming a Slope

A slope that's too steep to mow is frequently too steep to maintain as a garden. Although some sturdy plants will survive on a bank, most will need some help from stone, contoured terraces, or another device to hold the slope and restrain or channel the water following heavy rains. Managing the flow of rainwater is your biggest challenge, since unrestrained water will erode an incline as it rushes downward toward lower elevations.

In addition to reducing erosion, thoughtful landscaping of your slope will make it an easier place to work. In newly developed areas, the smooth banks left behind by bulldozers make for treacherous footing. Build some level terraces into your slope so that you will have solid places to stand and work. Be sure to choose low-maintenance plants that are suited to your site. Ground cover is useful in controlling erosion, as is a stone wall planted with easy-care rock garden plants. Weeding or pruning on a slope requires a certain amount of climbing and balancing, which you'll want to keep to a minimum. Make the lower parts of your slope as sturdy as possible so that you can use them as platforms when the higher tiers need your attention. 🌸

CREATING A ROCK GARDEN

Since rocks tumble naturally down a hill, a low rock wall that restrains the bottom of a slope looks as if it belongs there. If you build a dry wall without bonding cement, you can plant phlox, sedums, and other rock-garden plants in carefully prepared pockets. The materials below will make a 20-foot-long wall 18 inches high. You can reduce the materials proportionally for a smaller area. Have landscaping stone delivered close to the site. ❧

HAVE ON HAND:

- ▶ Five 12-inch wooden stakes
- ▶ Hammer
- ▶ String
- ▶ Shovel
- ▶ Wheelbarrow
- ▶ 200 pounds gravel
- ▶ Sturdy work gloves
- ▶ Landscaping stones, 1 ton
- ▶ 80 pounds dry peat moss
- ▶ 50-pound bag sand (if needed)

Use stakes and string to mark the location of your wall. Make it as straight as possible. Unnecessary contours will weaken the wall.

Use a shovel to dig a 14-inch-deep shelf into the slope. Set aside topsoil, rocks, and infertile subsoil in separate piles.

Dig the base by excavating 4 inches of soil from the bottom of the shelf. Make the front of the base 2 inches higher than the back.

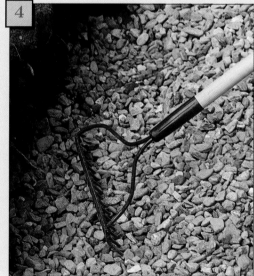

Spread a 3-inch layer of gravel on the excavated shelf. Contour gravel if needed to keep the lip 2 inches higher than the back.

Set your largest, flattest stones on gravel, slanting them backward so the fronts are slightly higher than the backs. Set firmly in place.

Mix equal parts of topsoil and peat moss to make planting mixture. Add sand to clay soil. Pack mixture firmly into crevices.

Place plants in largest crevices. Cover roots with planting mixture. Water well to dampen roots and planting mixture.

Repeat Steps 5-7 to complete wall. Use long stones for second layer. Set stones so the wall tilts back slightly toward the slope.

Mix equal parts of small stones or gravel with the planting mixture. Firmly pack into pockets left between wall and slope.

Set plants in the bed you have created between wall and slope. Water thoroughly. Mulch with a 2-inch layer of small stones and gravel.

Alternatives

GROUND COVER

Many of the best ground-cover plants for slopes become invasive when grown in less rugged situations. However, the rigors of growing on sloping land act as a restraint on such rapid spreaders as English ivy and periwinkle. You can use ground covers such as these alone, in combination with bulbs, or you can flank them with low evergreen shrubs, such as creeping junipers. Large swaths of the same plant will give a slope the most natural look.

If the bank is badly eroded and consists mostly of rocks and subsoil, dig planting pockets twice as large as the rootballs of your plants and fill them with high-quality topsoil. Thoroughly dampen your plants before you remove them from their pots. Plant them slightly deeper than they grew in their containers.

As you set out your ground-cover plants, also install a fabric or straw mulch to control weeds and erosion while the plants are getting established. Landscape fabric covered with a decorative mulch of pine needles suppresses weeds and allows rain to soak into the soil beneath it. However, avoid using it if your ground cover grows by putting down surface roots.

TERRACE

A terrace is a nearly level plateau built into a slope. Since water flows more slowly over a level surface, a terrace or series of terraces reduces erosion by slowing down rushing water. If your house is built on steeply sloping land, consider building a terrace to expand your usable outdoor space and help channel the flow of water around your house. Consult a professional first; this can be a big job.

The best place for a terrace is on the low side of your house. When planning, keep in mind that the area just below the terrace will receive copious amounts of water following heavy rains. To avoid creating an erosion problem, rock-lined conduits for water runoff can be built, either by you or by a contractor.

You may need stones to hold the edges of reinforcing timbers in place. Concrete retaining-wall blocks that are made to look like stone are easy to install and are also effective. To stabilize terrace edges with landscape timbers, they must be anchored into the slope with a perpendicular tie, called a deadman. This is best done by an experienced contractor.

Masking Tree Bases

With a little planning and preparation, you can create a beautiful carpet of plants at the bases of your mature trees that will look great all season long. Shallow soil, too much shade, or competition for water and nutrients may have discouraged plants from getting established under your trees in the past. Working with these conditions, not against them, is your key to achieving the lush, finished look you want.

Since the area under your trees' canopies will be shady for a good portion of the day, choose plants that thrive in a shady location. Consider also that shade from different kinds of trees can vary. Evergreen trees, for example, cast deep shade all year round. Deciduous trees create varying amounts of shade. A large-leaved tree, such as a magnolia, will shade the area beneath it almost completely for most of the day. A tree with small, finely cut leaves, such as a Japanese maple, will create dappled shade beneath it.

Whether your choice is a planted ground cover, a moss bed, spring bulbs, or mulch, masking the bases of some of your trees will add unexpected interest to your landscape. 🌺

INSTALLING GROUND COVER

Ground covers are used to create a carpet of lush green foliage and flowers. Many plant species work well in this capacity. Some excellent choices include hosta, ivy, pachysandra, ferns, bergenia, and periwinkle.

Follow the closest spacing requirements for the plants you choose, and fill the area with plants to create a dense ground cover. Plants need only enough room to grow and flourish; close planting will give you the best visual effect and will also conserve water and discourage weeds by completely shading the soil surface. 🌿

HAVE ON HAND:

▶ Grass rake

▶ Topsoil (if needed)

▶ Balanced 10-10-10 fertilizer (nitrogen, phosphorus, potassium)

▶ Hand spade

▶ Watering can or garden sprinkler

▶ Edger

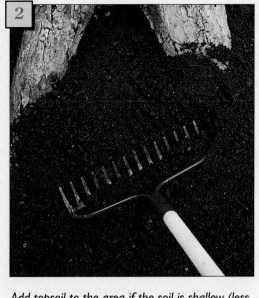

1
Rake away dead leaves, remove stones and debris from the area to be planted. Try not to disturb tree roots that may be near the surface.

2
Add topsoil to the area if the soil is shallow (less than 3 inches) at the base of the tree. Level soil with back of rake.

3
Broadcast a slow-release, balanced fertilizer such as 10-10-10 to nourish your developing plants as they begin to take hold.

4
Begin planting close to tree base, working out toward edge of bed. Use a hand spade to dig holes, moving slowly so as not to damage roots.

Set the young plants just below the surrounding soil surface so that a water-collecting depression is created around the plant base.

Plant in a triangular pattern for the best effect and maximum coverage, keeping recommended spacing in mind as you work.

Once your plants are in the ground, mulch and water them thoroughly to help settle the soil around plant roots without disturbing them.

Spreading lime or flour, mark bed's perimeter evenly, then follow with a long-handled garden edger to tidy appearance.

HERE'S HOW

HOW MANY PLANTS?

You can easily calculate the number of ground-cover plants you will need for a given area. Begin by measuring the bed to be planted. Next, calculate the bed's square footage. Then divide that number by the individual square footage requirements of the plants you intend to use. For example, some hostas require 2-foot spacing. To determine how many hostas you need, divide the total square footage of your bed by two. The number you arrive at is the number of plants needed to fill the area completely.

Alternatives

MOSS

Nothing rivals the serenity of an emerald green carpet of moss. Establishing a moss garden at the base of a mature tree takes prior preparation but, once established, it is virtually trouble-free. Moss is a good solution for an area under a tree where there is not enough topsoil because tree roots grow close to the surface.

Moss needs acid soil, so test the pH of the area where you will plant it; add gypsum or sulfur if the soil is not acidic. Because moss is not available in plant nurseries, look for it growing in your area. You can collect moss from its natural habitat as long as you leave some behind so the bed can reestablish itself. Lift it in sheets and keep it moist by wrapping in damp newspaper until you can plant it in your yard. Then place the moss on clean, cleared ground and press into the dirt with the palm of your hand. Don't be gentle; you want the moss to make solid contact with the soil surface so it won't dry out. The key word in moss gardening is water—and plenty of it.

Water your moss garden every day for a few weeks. Don't allow it to dry out completely. Maintain by removing leaves that fall upon it in autumn.

BULBS

Planting bulbs at the base of a tree in your landscape creates a beautiful splash of color and contrast, often before other plants in the garden have gotten started for the season. Spring bulbs emerge early, before deciduous trees have leafed out, and so get plenty of the direct sunlight they need.

For best results with your bulbs, add a phosphorus-rich fertilizer to the soil, such as bone meal or any of the commercial formulations recommended for bulbs. This increases the longevity of the planting and ensures that your bulbs will return year after year.

When planting spring-flowering bulbs in the fall, resist the temptation to form a perfect ring around the tree. Instead, scatter them unevenly among the tree's roots, taking care not to damage the roots. Doing this will give the planting a more natural appearance.

The list of bulbs you can use is nearly endless. Familiarize yourself with the wide assortment of tulips, daffodils, hyacinths, crocus, and scillas available from nurseries and garden catalogs. All do well in most soil types. Also, try some of the more unusual bulbs such as fritillaria, anemone, and cyclamen for a satisfying spring garden at the base of your tree.

Designing for a Wet Site

THIS GARDEN THRIVES WITH

SUN	WATER	SOIL
Sun to shade	**High**	**Average**

A wet spot in your landscape presents an opportunity to grow and enjoy a number of beautiful plants that you can't grow in ordinary, well-drained garden soil. Some species not only tolerate poorly drained soil but actually need the constant moisture in order to thrive. By planning your design around such plants, you can turn a potentially challenging area into a beautiful landscape asset.

When choosing plants for a wet site, keep in mind that some need full sun while others prefer a shady location. Check the amount of sunlight available in all parts of your wet site before deciding on your plant list. For the most attractive effect, include a mixture of different flowers, plant forms, and foliage shapes or textures. Placing such bold, upright plants as irises next to graceful, mounded plants, such as hostas, shows each off to its best advantage.

Other landscape features can be incorporated into this design for added interest. If your site does not already have standing water for much of the year, you can easily install a pond liner to create a shallow pool. Large rocks are a natural accompaniment to water features and lush, moisture-loving plants. Carefully chosen, weatherproof sculptures can also make attractive garden accents. ❦

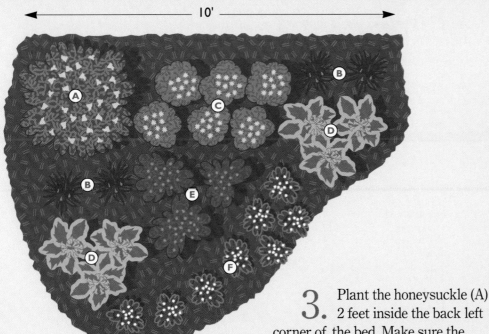

← 10' →

PLANT LIST

A. Honeysuckle, 1, 7 feet tall

B. Japanese iris, 4, 2 to 3 feet tall

C. Solomon's seal, 6, 2 to 3 feet tall

D. Hosta undulata, 'Univittata', 6,
2 feet tall

E. Wild blue phlox, 3, 18 inches tall

F. Foamflower, 8, 10 inches tall

(See next page for more on plants.)

1. Relatively dry soil is easier to mix with soil amendments, so wait for dry weather to landscape your wet site. Meanwhile, remove weeds, rocks, and other debris from the site. Prune off excess low limbs from nearby trees to promote good light penetration and air circulation. Be sure to leave enough shade for plants that prefer it.

2. Cultivate the soil 12 inches deep, and work in a 3-inch layer of humus such as compost, leaf mold, or peat moss. If you have clay soil, also add a 1-inch layer of coarse sand. Place a board in the center of the bed so you will have a clean place to stand while you set out the plants.

3. Plant the honeysuckle (A) 2 feet inside the back left corner of the bed. Make sure the tops of the roots are covered with 1 inch of soil. In the right back corner of the bed, plant two irises (B), spaced 8 inches apart. Fill the center back of the bed with two rows of Solomon's seal (C), spaced 10 inches apart. Set three hostas (D) along the right side of the bed so they will shade the roots of the iris.

4. Move the board forward and fill the center of the bed with blue phlox (E), arranged in a triangular pattern. Plant the remaining irises and hostas as shown. Place foamflowers (F) in a loose curve in the front of the bed as shown.

5. Thoroughly water all plants and mulch them with 2 inches of organic material.

HERE'S HOW

CREATE AN INVITING SITE

Make your wet site an attractive retreat by adding mulch or gravel walkways that skirt the garden's edge. If you place benches or rustic boards across stone supports along the walkway or by the edges of the garden, they will invite the casual stroller to stop and enjoy the view.

Plants for a Wet, Shady Site

The plants listed here are all excellent choices for a garden in a wet site. All are perennials, so they will come back year after year without replanting and will increase in size with time.

These plants, which do well in light to partial shade, will create a staggered sequence of color so your garden will be interesting from early spring through fall. Variations in height and foliage ensure appeal even between bloom times.

If your site is only seasonally wet, you may have to supplement natural rainfall to keep the soil from drying out. Water whenever the top inch or two of soil feels dry.

To help your garden always look its best, use pruners to deadhead blooms as they fade and remove any yellowed leaves or weeds. 🌺

HONEYSUCKLE
Lonicera tatarica
7 feet tall
Zones 3-9
Pale pink to white flowers in spring, red berries in fall; deciduous, green leaves; average, moist soil; full/part sun; high water. Can be invasive.

JAPANESE IRIS
Iris laevigata
2-3 feet tall
Zones 3-9
Bluish-purple or white flowers, early summer; tall, smooth, narrow foliage; average, moist soil; sun/part shade; high water. Thrives in moist conditions or shallow water

SOLOMON'S SEAL
Polygonatum biflorum
2-3 feet tall
Zones 3-9
Yellowish white flowers, early spring; small, oval leaves; fertile, moist, well-drained soil; shade; high water. Likes a cool, shady site. Divide in early spring. Some varieties fragrant.

HOSTA UNDULATA
Hosta undulata
2 feet tall
Zones 4-9
Lavender flowers, midsummer; wavy, white-and-green leaves in clumps; moist, neutral soil; shade; medium water. Divide in spring.

WILD BLUE PHLOX
Phlox divarica
18 inches tall
Zones 3-8
Saucer-shaped, lavender-blue blooms, early summer; small oval leaves; moist, well-drained soil; part shade; medium water. Forms mats.

FOAMFLOWER
Tiarella wherryi
10 inches tall
Zones 4-8
Star-shaped, white or pink flowers in spring; hairy green leaves; moist, well-drained soil; deep shade; medium water. Divide in spring.

CARE FOR YOUR WET SITE GARDEN

SPRING Clean up your wet site garden by raking away dead leaves and yard debris. Replace winter mulch with a new layer to help plants retain moisture. Divide hostas, solomon's seal, iris, and foamflower as needed.

SUMMER Clip off spent blooms regularly, and lightly prune honeysuckle after the flowers fade. Keep the garden free of weeds. Water during periods of drought as needed. Keep an eye out for other plants to include in next year's garden.

FALL After the first hard frost, remove the dead foliage from hostas with hand pruners. Rake up leaves after they fall from nearby trees and renew mulch so the garden is neat during the winter, which will discourage overwintering of pests. 🌺

Alternative

NATIVE PLANTS FOR WET, SUNNY SITES

Plants that are native to stream banks and open wetlands in your climate usually have a high level of resistance to the soil-borne fungal diseases that cause the roots of many cultivated plants to rot. When seeking native plants to use in sunny, wet sections of your landscape, study the species that most often grow near area ponds and bogs. Several native plants adapted to wet, sunny spots are now widely available at nurseries. If you like their appearance, also consider using some plants that are often regarded as wayside weeds, such as swamp milkweed, mallows, ironweed, and grassy-looking sedges. If you want to make these wildlings look like cultivated plants, arrange them in informal groups, with open areas between them. A mulched path or board-walk will turn the planting into a lovely garden.

You can anchor your wet site with these or other native plants and use nonnatives for seasonal color. For example, cannas are a popular color plant for wet sun in warm climates. Where winters are colder, coreopsis and other annual wildflowers make good summer companions for native shrubs. You can also plant willows in wet sun provided their extensive roots will not interfere with buried water pipes. ❧

JOE-PYE WEED
Eupatorium maculatum
3-5 feet tall
Zones 4-9
Dense, thistle-like, light purple flowers, late summer; light green, coarse, oval leaves; moist, well-drained soil; full sun/part shade; medium water. Divide in early spring or autumn.

WINTERBERRY
Ilex verticillata
7 feet tall
Zones 4-9
Deciduous, saw-toothed, bright green leaves; brilliant red winter berries; young branches are purplish green; acidic soil; full/part sun; medium water.. Can be grown as small tree. Female plants produce berries; male plant needed for pollination.

BEE BALM
Monarda didyma
2-3 feet tall
Zones 4-8
Vivid scarlet-red flowers on square stems, late summer; oval, hairy leaves; moist, well-drained soil; sun/part shade; high water. Grows wild in wet places, thickets, and the banks of streams.

BUGBANE
Cimicifuga racemosa
6 feet tall
Zones 3-9
Tall spikes of pure white flowers, midsummer; broad, oval, finely divided leaves; average, moist soil; sun/light shade; medium water. Very graceful appearance. Also known as black cohosh or black snakeroot.

CRANBERRY BUSH
Viburnum trilobum
10 feet tall
Zones 2-7
Showy white flowers, late spring; coarsely toothed leaves; arching clusters of shiny red berries throughout winter; moist, fertile soil; sun/part shade; high water. Cut out older shoots after flowering. Attractive to birds.

Landscaping for Deep Shade

THIS GARDEN THRIVES WITH

SUN	WATER	SOIL
Deep shade	**High**	**Well drained**

You can bring structure, light, and visual interest to shady spots by filling them with plants that prefer partial to deep shade. All plants need light to grow, but those that are adapted to shade grow best in light that is filtered through tree foliage or blocked by buildings during much of the day.

Leaf texture and variegation play leading roles in the shade garden, for most shade plants are not exuberant bloomers. Plants with light-colored leaves brighten dark places, and those with ferny foliage create soft accents. Foliage plants such as hostas, caladiums, ferns, and coleus are always welcome additions to the shade garden. You can use ground-cover plants to give the ground level of your shade garden a finished appearance. Add seasonal color with shade-loving summer annuals.

Many shady locations have problems such as poorly drained soil or a thick layer of tree roots just below the soil's surface. It's important to improve planting sites for your landscape plants by amending the soil with plenty of organic matter. If the soil is difficult to dig, you can grow many shade-tolerant plants in attractively arranged containers. ❦

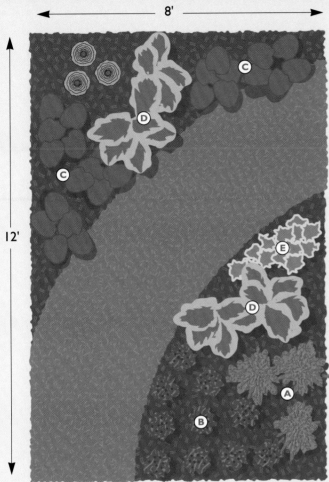

8'

12'

PLANT LIST

A. Astilbe, 3, 30 to 36 inches tall

B. Sweet violet, 10, 6 to 8 inches tall

C. Hosta 'Elegans', 5, 2 feet tall

D. Hosta 'Frances Williams', 4, 3 feet tall

E. Hosta, 'Shade Master', 1, 18 inches tall

(See next page for more on plants.)

3. Dig planting areas 14 inches deep on both sides of pathway, working around large tree roots. Mix a 4- to 6-inch layer of peat moss, compost, or other organic matter into the planting areas. Rake smooth.

4. Place boards on top of prepared soil and stand on them while planting three astilbes (A) 18 inches apart in the section of bed farthest from path.

5. Stand on boards if necessary to plant 10 sweet violets (B) 8 inches apart. Set violets at least 6 inches in from edge of the pathway.

6. Plant all hostas (C, D, E). Space hostas 2 feet apart and set them at least 1 foot in from the edge of the path-way. Water and mulch all plants.

7. Bury edges of the landscape fab-ric and mulch over pathway with pine needles, shredded bark, or light-colored pebbles.

1. Open the overhead canopy by pruning away low tree limbs and trimming nearby bushes. Rake area clean of fallen leaves and debris.

2. Fill in any low spots in pathway that may retain water after heavy rains. Rake center of pathway level, allowing a slight grade on the sides to improve drainage. Lay porous landscape fabric over the pathway.

HERE'S HOW

LAYING GRAVEL PATHS

Pathways paved with light-colored pebbles help brighten up shady places. They are also less likely to host slugs, a common leaf-eating pest in damp, shady situations. Line the bottom of your path with landscape fabric and bury the edges before adding pebbles. For firmer footing, place flat stepping-stones on the fabric and surround them with pea gravel.

Perennials for Shade

Sometimes known as shade lilies, hostas are among the easiest shade plants to grow. Small cultivars can be used as summer ground covers, and those with variegated or tinted leaves bring much needed contrast to the shade garden. Hostas die back to the ground after the first hard frost, and new leaves emerge from pointed leaf buds in the spring. The plants reach full size about three years after planting. Hosta roots are tough and fleshy and transplant easily. You can expand your hosta collection by cutting mature clumps apart with a sharp shovel in early spring and immediately replanting them.

In this shade garden, the filigreed leaves and feathery tops of astilbes provide textural interest, while little violets bring a touch of color and fragrance and help complete the impression of a cool woodland glade.

Protect your shade garden from deer and slugs. ❧

ASTILBE
Astilbe x arendsii
30 to 36 inches tall
Zone 4
White, pink, red, or lavender plumes, summer, will repeat if trimmed; finely cut foliage; well-drained soil; shade; high water.

SWEET VIOLET
Viola odorata
6 to 8 inches tall
Zone 6
Purple, white, or pink, fragrant flowers, spring; foliage dark green and heart-shaped; well-drained soil; shade; high water. Requires little attention once established.

HOSTA
Hosta sieboldiana 'Elegans'
2 feet tall
Zone 3
White flowers on tall stalks, midsummer; leaves large and broad, blue-green and symmetrically furrowed; well-drained soil; shade; high water. Full, mounding habit. Easy to grow.

HOSTA
Hosta sieboldiana 'Frances Williams'
3 feet tall
Zone 3
Lavender flowers on tall stalks, mid-summer, broad, blue-green, slightly puckered leaves edged with yellow; well-drained soil; shade; high water. Flowers attract hummingbirds.

HOSTA
Hosta undulata 'Shade Master'
3 feet tall
Zone 3
Lavender flowers on tall stalks, mid-summer; broad, wavy, lime-green leaves; well-drained soil; shade; high water. A high contrast hosta.

CARE FOR YOUR SHADE GARDEN

SPRING Pull winter weeds and trim any damaged limbs and twigs from nearby trees and shrubs. Spread a 1-inch layer of weed-free compost or composted manure over plants. Renew mulch in pathway.

SUMMER After perennials are up and growing, place a 2-inch layer of fresh mulch around them. Trim withered blossoms as needed and pull weeds as they appear. Plant shade-loving annuals for extra summer color.

FALL Cut foliage off at ground level after it is killed by cold weather. Remove any tree leaves that fall on plants. After ground freezes, lay evergreen boughs over the crowns of perennials to prevent soil heaving. ❧

Alternative

ACCENT PLANTS FOR SHADE

You can get a good look at nature's idea of a great shade garden by studying a forest floor. Tiny ground-cover plants creep around tree bases, ferns pop out from rocks and banks, and most of the plants that bloom do so in spring, when there's still a bit of winter sun coming through bare tree branches.

You can follow nature's blueprint in your shade garden by using ground covers, hardy ferns, and shrubs that are naturally at home in the woods. If you're a plant collector at heart, the shade garden is a perfect place to experiment with perennial woodland wildflowers such as columbines and foamflowers. Like hostas and astilbes, all shade plants grow best in soil that has been enriched with organic matter to make it resemble the soft soil of a forest floor. Mulches help keep the soil moist and cool in summer.

Try adding shade-loving annual flowers for cool summer color. If your shade garden is already filled with hostas and other perennials, grow your annuals in containers or in baskets hung from the branches of trees. Choose flowers with white or light pastel blooms to brighten even your darkest corner. ❦

WOOD FERN
Dryopteris spp.
2 feet tall
Zone 4
Airy fronds persist through winter; needs especially well-drained soil; shade; constant soil moisture. Plants form clumps. Outstanding texture. Most species are evergreen.

LILY-OF-THE-VALLEY
Convallaria majalis
10 inches tall
Zone 3
Dainty spikes of tiny, fragrant cup-shaped, white flowers, spring; sword-shaped, upright green leaves; well-drained soil; shade; high water. Plants quickly multiply to form close ground cover.

COLEUS
Coleus hybrids
18 inches tall
All zones
Small, blue flowers, late-summer; less attractive than vividly colored leaves in red, pink, white, yellow, and green shades; well-drained soil; shade; high water. Summer annual.

RHODODENDRON
Rhododendron spp.
2-10 feet tall
Zone 4
Clumps of, pink, white, or red flowers in spring; evergreen, leathery leaves curl in below-freezing weather; well-drained, acid soil; shade; high water. Plant high to prevent root rot. Keep well mulched.

IMPATIENS
Impatiens wallerana hybrids
1 foot tall
All zones
Flowers in dozens of shades, including bicolors and soft pastels; green leaves; well-drained soil; shade; high water. Excellent in containers or use as mounded edging plant. Summer annual.

Tackling the Elements

Y ou can alter fundamental characteristics of your yard to make it more comfortable for you and your family. Blocking excessive wind, adding shady pockets to sun-drenched areas, or installing barriers to make your outdoor space more private enhance the value of your property by making your land more usable and attractive. Adding shade or windbreaks can also reduce the costs of cooling and heating your home.

Before you begin any of these projects, take some time to study the problem you are trying to solve. Refer to your landscape map to make sure the changes you make fit logically into the ways you plan to use your outdoor space. Plan ahead for pathways, play areas, and special gardens you may want to add later. Preserve the most desirable views, and make sure any structures you add are properly scaled to the size of your house and other large features in your landscape.

Whether you are bringing shade to sunny areas or slowing down the wind as it sweeps across your yard, the changes you make will create new environments for different types of plants. This diversity can strengthen the health and appeal of your landscape by attracting a vast assortment of birds, butterflies, and other wild companions. ✿

Creating Shade

Cool pockets of shade improve a landscape's appearance, provide comfortable spots to relax, and create places to grow plants that would rather not spend their days in full sun. Shady areas near the south or west sides of your house, where sunlight is most intense, can also make your home easier to cool in the summer.

The most natural way to create shade is to plant a tree, but some years must pass before a young tree will grow large enough to provide significant shade. Meanwhile, you can create a shady nook or passageway by building a pergola, an arbor with an open horizontal roof supported by columns or posts. This type of structure can be made from many different materials, including tree timbers, sapling poles, bamboo, split logs, or pre-cut lumber. Unlike gazebos and other structures with roofs, pergolas allow rain and filtered sun to reach the plants growing beneath them.

In terms of landscape design, a pergola can work as a visual accent by itself, or it can link the house to special landscape features such as a colorful border or pond. It's also a great way to cool a sunny pathway that connects different gardens within the same yard. ❧

VINE-COVERED PERGOLA

This structure, built from standard lengths of lumber, can be painted for a formal look, or you can stain and seal it to create a more rustic mood. A bench can be built into the side of the pergola, or you can enjoy the filtered shade with portable seating.

Good plant possibilities for your pergola include climbing roses, clematis, grapes, honeysuckle, and trumpet vine. 🐾

HAVE ON HAND:

- ▶ Tape measure
- ▶ Four 1-foot-long stakes
- ▶ Hammer
- ▶ Posthole digger
- ▶ Shovel
- ▶ Four posts: 10-foot-long 4 x 4s
- ▶ Carpenter's level
- ▶ String
- ▶ Pencil
- ▶ Two lower side supports: 44-inch-long 2 x 4s
- ▶ Box of 16d galvanized nails
- ▶ Saw
- ▶ Two upper side supports: 48-inch-long 2 x 4s
- ▶ Two rafters: 8-foot-long 2 x 4s
- ▶ Nine top strips: 4-foot-long 2 x 2s

Mark the positions of the two back posts with stakes spaced 80 inches apart. Place stakes for front posts 42 inches from back post stakes.

Measure between diagonal corners to make sure the stakes create a perfect square. The two diagonal measurements should be the same.

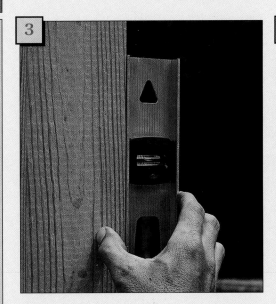

Dig holes for posts 18 inches deep. Set posts in holes. Partially refill holes, using level to be sure uprights are straight. Finish refilling post holes.

Run a string around posts 16 inches from the ground, leaving front open. Check to be sure string is level and mark line on inside of posts.

Position lower side supports inside posts along level marks, checking again to make sure posts are straight and supports are level. Nail in place.

Run a level string between the tops of the posts as in Step 4. Saw tops of posts even. Run another level string 6 inches from tops of posts. Mark.

Attach upper side supports as in Step 5. Center the rafters atop the ends of side supports, on the outside of the posts. Nail rafters to posts.

Lay top strips across rafters, with end strips 1 inch inside ends of rafters, and others evenly spaced about 1 foot apart. Nail in place.

HERE'S HOW

SET POSTS IN CONCRETE

Even if you use treated wood, posts that are set in the ground eventually will rot. In addition, some soils are so light that they will not hold the posts firmly upright, even when they are set very deeply. Setting posts in concrete solves both of these problems.

Vibrations from nailing and sawing can ruin concrete footers, so use pieces of scrap lumber to brace poles in place while you are building your pergola, and fill the holes with concrete when your structure is complete.

Alternatives

USING TREES

The best shade trees, maples and oaks for instance, are deciduous: They will provide shelter from the sun in summer but allow the winter sun to filter through after they drop their leaves. Oaks grow steadily; several kinds may grow as much as two feet per year. Different kinds of maples have various growth rates. Check with your local nursery or Cooperative Extension Service for expert advice on shade trees appropriate for your area and their rates of growth.

Avoid planting trees such as hickories or mulberries that drop nuts or fruit. Their fallout may encourage animals or stain your walkways. However, some people enjoy the birds that are attracted to mulberry trees. Also, think carefully before planting pines, cedars, or other evergreen trees. Some are fast growers and will do a wonderful job of screening quickly but eventually cast so much shade that it is often impossible to grow anything in their shadows.

Planting shade trees is best done in late winter or early spring. Give your transplanted trees extra water their first year. Cover root zones with a mulch to discourage weeds and grasses and to eliminate the need for close mowing that might damage the main trunks. ❦

USING YOUR HOUSE

You can create a delightfully shady spot just outside your house by building a modified pergola that extends the line of your roof over a patio and uses the side of your house as a windbreak. In addition to creating a comfortable bower from which you can enjoy the outdoors, a pergola will add to the permanent value and attractiveness of your home.

Shade can also be created in small courtyards, patios, and pool areas by attaching a canvas overhang to the eaves of your house. Canvas shades are usually taken down and stored during the winter even if you choose a fabric that is relatively rot- and mildewproof. You can make shades appear more permanent by securing them in summer to sturdy posts, perhaps of painted wood or iron, and attaching the canvas corners with the help of hooks and grommets. A local company that makes custom draperies might be able to help you with this sewing job.

A pergola constructed with treated wood will last a great deal longer than canvas shades and can be made into a charming extension of your garden. You can choose plants to grow overhead, perhaps climbing roses or wisteria, to create a beautiful, shady bower to enjoy all season long. ❦

Installing a Decorative Barrier

The decorative barrier at left brings visual structure to an artful grouping of flowers and shrubs and helps frame the rest of the landscape at the same time. Installed in a corner of your garden or along the edge of your property, a short section of rustic fence defines boundaries while imparting a relaxed, pastoral mood. If your landscape looks a little too formal, a corner framed in weathered wood will lend a feeling of cozy warmth. This landscaping trick creates the illusion of enclosure while also preserving the impression of spaciousness.

Decorative barriers can fulfill practical landscape purposes, too. A short section of ornamental fence will direct the flow of foot traffic around delicate perennials, which should not be trod upon while they are dormant. Fencing can also serve as a secure trellis for prickly plants such as climbing roses. Perennial vines that need regular pruning to keep them well behaved, like trumpet vine or wisteria, are ideal candidates for fencepost planting. If a low-maintenance plan is more to your liking, flank your fence with a symmetrical group of junipers or other elegant evergreens for year-round drama and beauty. ❧

WOODEN FENCE

This 16-foot-long, post-and-rail, angled corner fence can be built using precut materials purchased at building supply stores. The rail pieces come in 8-foot sections. Try to find posts and rails made from cedar, which resists termites and weathers to a light gray color. If you wish, you can use these instructions to make a longer, straight fence instead of an angled-corner one. ❧

HAVE ON HAND:

- ▶ Three 1-foot stakes
- ▶ Hammer
- ▶ Four horizontal rails
- ▶ Posthole digger
- ▶ Tarp
- ▶ One corner post
- ▶ Two end posts
- ▶ Three heavyweight garbage bags
- ▶ Six thick rubber bands
- ▶ Shovel
- ▶ Carpenter's level
- ▶ 50-pound bag gravel
- ▶ Scissors

Drive a stake into the ground where the corner post will be placed. Lay two rails on the ground at right angles from the stake.

Drive stakes into the ground where the end posts will be placed. Remove the side rails from your work area.

Dig the hole for the corner post 2 feet deep and 1 foot wide. Set the excavated dirt on a tarp for use in later steps.

Place plastic garbage bags around post bottoms. Secure the bags to the posts with rubber bands placed 8 and 18 inches from the bottoms.

Place the corner post in the hole, turning it so the side holes face the end posts. Refill the hole with enough soil to hold the post straight.

Check location of end posts again by holding opposing side rails in place. Dig holes for the end posts, as in Step 3.

Assemble all pieces. Use the carpenter's level to make sure posts are straight. If needed, level side rails by adjusting the depth of end posts.

Refill holes with soil and gravel. Pack soil firmly around the posts with the handle end of your shovel. Trim off exposed edges of plastic bags.

HERE'S HOW

FINISH UNDER THE FENCE

If parts of your wood fence are anchored in grass, plan ahead to avoid tedious mowing and weed trimming around the bases of the posts. Before grass has a chance to grow around the posts, circle them with rounds of landscape fabric. You can also use a strip of landscape fabric to cover the area under the fence that is not used for ornamental plants. Mulch over the fabric with shredded bark, pine needles, or pretty stones. Small ground-cover plants such as ajuga and liriope can also be used as attractive, low-maintenance finishes under your fence.

Alternatives

HEDGE

The formal look of a hedge makes a lovely decorative barrier for many older homes. Historically, hedges have been used to emphasize boundaries between public spaces and private ones, and to create walls for outdoor rooms. If you are restoring an old house or cultivating a look of classic elegance for a new one, you may be happiest with a hedge.

Study hedge plants that do well in your area, and check with local nurseries to find the best cultivars. Many of the newer hedge plants resist common diseases and stop growing at specific sizes, so they require much less care than older cultivars.

When installing a new hedge, buy extra plants and keep them growing in large pots through the first winter. That way, if a plant from your original planting fails to grow or becomes badly damaged, you will have an exact match to plug into the space left in your hedge.

To shape your hedge, angle the sides out slightly so that the base is a little wider than the top. This will enable light to reach the lowest branches. The result will be more even growth. 🌼

WROUGHT-IRON FENCING

Small courtyards, patios, and other limited areas where every detail is important are ideal spots for elegant wrought-iron fences. While wrought iron is most familiar as an architectural detail, it can also be used very effectively as an ornamental accent in your landscape. You can also use small panels of wrought-iron fencing to create a lovely barrier along a narrow walkway in your side yard. Or dress up a modest entryway by edging its approach with a low run of decorative wrought iron.

Wrought iron is heavy and must be set in concrete if it is to hold up well to wind and wet weather. In addition to having an assistant help as you set the fencing in wet concrete, you will need to build a temporary reinforcing frame from inexpensive pine lumber to hold the wrought iron in place for two or three days, or until the concrete dries hard.

Ornamental vines make beautiful partners for wrought iron, but they must be able to withstand severe pruning from time to time, when the iron needs repainting. Especially in warm, damp climates, wrought iron can be counted upon to need some kind of maintenance every two or three years.🌼

Establishing a Windbreak

If you live in a region where strong winds blow persistently, you can screen and protect your house and landscape by planting a windbreak. Wind increases the effects of high or low temperatures and robs plants of much-needed water in summer and winter. A windbreak reduces stress on landscape plants and makes your garden a more comfortable place for you and your family.

Since most windbreaks are situated where they will soften winter winds and block blowing snow, small- to medium-sized evergreen trees are the best plants for the job. You can space evergreen trees closely together to form a solid green wall that blocks an unwanted view, or you may want to allow more space between the trees so that they filter strong winds and frame a panoramic scene. Avoid using brittle trees such as tall, top-heavy pines, which are likely to split as they mature.

Planning will make your windbreak more effective. Determine prevailing winds by tying ribbons to several 4-foot-tall stakes on your property. A windbreak should buffer the wind at approximately a right angle to wind direction, but you can adjust the placement so that it not only buffers wind but also works well with the rest of your landscape. ✿

THIS GARDEN THRIVES WITH

SUN	WATER	SOIL
Full	Medium	Average

1. Choose a location for your wind-break at least 25 feet upwind of the area you wish to protect. Place stakes in the ground at the center and at both ends of a 50-foot line along your planned windbreak. Tie taut string between stakes. Tie short pieces of ribbon or cloth strips to the string at 8-foot intervals to mark planting holes for arborvitae.

2. Dig planting holes for the arborvitae (A) as deep as the plants' rootballs and twice as wide. Place plants in the planting holes and remove wires and wrapping material. Adjust soil beneath the plants as need-ed to make them stand straight at the same depth they grew in the field. Backfill with soil halfway; flood the holes with water and wait for it to seep in. Finish backfilling with soil. Mulch with a 3-inch layer of wood chips.

3. Plant 6 creeping junipers (B) in a line 10 feet in front of the arborvitae. Center the junipers in the spaces between the arborvitae. Install a sheet mulch of perforated plastic or landscape fabric on both sides of the junipers. Cover the sheet mulch with a 3-inch layer of wood chips.

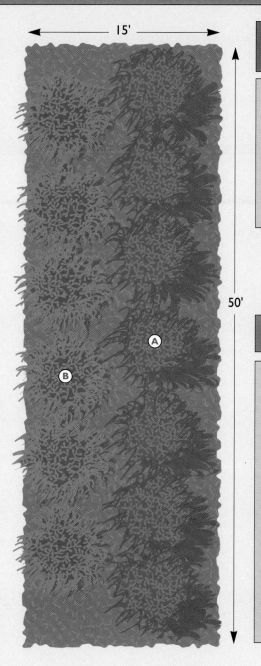

15'

50'

PLANT LIST

A. Arborvitae, 7, 6 to 25 feet tall

B. Creeping juniper, 6,
6 to 20 inches tall

(See next page for more on plants.)

HERE'S HOW

DRIP WATER FROM JUGS

To create a slow water drip to your windbreak plants, make two small holes in the sides of plastic milk jugs, 2 inches from the bottoms of the jugs. Fill with water and place above root zones of the plants. The water left in the jugs below the holes will keep them from blowing away.

Plants for a Windbreak

Arborvitae is a slow grower, but its fine texture and formal structure make it an excellent windbreak plant. You can plant arborvitae in the spring or in the fall. It grows slowly the first year after planting, as it needs time to establish roots. Once established, arborvitae needs little care except for supplemental water during droughts. You can choose from many different cultivars of these tough and adaptable plants.

Creeping juniper makes a fine partner for more upright evergreens. Its branches spread from the main crown and do not develop roots along the low branches. Weed control is crucial, for junipers spread slowly at first. If you do not wish to use landscape fabric to suppress weeds, mulch your junipers with 3 inches of wheat or rye straw topped with a 2-inch layer of pine needles.

ARBORVITAE
Thuja occidentalis
6-25 feet tall
Zone 2
Flowers insignificant; flat panels of dense, needle-like evergreen foliage; moist, fertile soil; full sun; medium water. Formal, upright form in various shapes and heights.

CREEPING JUNIPER
Juniperus horizontalis
6-20 inches tall
Zone 3
Flowers insignificant; blue-green, needle-like evergreen foliage on spreading, woody branches; slightly acidic soil; full sun; medium water. Gray-blue berries in late summer.

SWISS STONE PINE
Pinus cembra
35 feet tall
Zone 4
Flowers insignificant; blue-green evergreen needles; slightly acidic soil; full sun; medium water, tolerates drought when established. Rounded pyramidal form; 3-inch cones.

LEYLAND CYPRESS
Cupressocyparis leylandii
to 60 feet tall
Zone 6
Flowers insignificant; blue-green evergreen needles on spreading branches; moist soil; full sun/part shade; heat tolerant and prunable. Attractive reddish bark.

CANADIAN HEMLOCK
Tsuga canadensis
40-70 feet tall
Zone 3
Flowers insignificant; dark green evergreen needles on spreading branches; any moist soil; full sun/slight shade; medium water. Strong pyramidal form; 1-inch cones.

CARE FOR YOUR WINDBREAK

SPRING Trim off broken branches or any winter-damaged limbs to maintain a neat and healthy appearance. Fertilize windbreak with acid plant fertilizer, following package instructions. Renew bark or wood chip mulch to retain soil moisture.

SUMMER Promptly pull out weeds that emerge near creeping junipers. Water all windbreak plants during severe droughts. Examine your arborvitae for signs of spider mites and bagworms. Heavy infestations may require a single pesticide treatment.

FALL Your windbreak will need little, if any, attention at the end of the season. Replace bare spots in the mulch with fresh material, and provide water to young plants if the weather is very dry.

Alternative

CREATING A HEDGEROW FOR WILDLIFE

If your property is too small for a windbreak of evergreen trees, you can use a hedgerow of shrubs to shelter your yard from strong winds. Noninvasive shrubs that produce berries can turn your windbreak into a bird sanctuary. Many of the same shrubs that provide food for birds also have flowers that attract beneficial insects.

Some shrubs that produce berries, such as privet, bush honeysuckle, or Russian olive, can quickly become pest plants. Since any berries that birds eat can sprout into widely scattered volunteer plants, the safest bird-friendly shrubs are native species that are not strong reseeders. Some of these are suggested here, and most of them provide the extra bonus of a display of vivid colors in the fall.

You can also combine evergreens and berry-producing shrubs in a windbreak or hedgerow. The evergreens provide nesting sites for birds, while the shrubs furnish food as well as habitat. Although a mixed planting of shrubs can look quite attractive by itself, deciduous shrubs that drop their leaves in winter look best when their limb structures, flowers, and fruits are displayed against an evergreen background. To create a natural look, group several of a similar plant together. 🌸

NINEBARK
Physocarpus spp.
5-9 feet tall
Zone 2
Small pink or white flowers, spring; reddish-brown fruit capsules, fall; foliage green; slightly acidic soil; mostly sun; medium water. Attractive, peeling bark.

WINTERBERRY
Ilex verticillata
8-10 feet tall
Zone 4
Greenish white flowers, spring, followed by bright red berries if male pollinator present; glossy, green, deciduous leaves; moist, mulched soil; sun/part shade; medium water.

CRANBERRY BUSH
Viburnum trilobum
10-15 feet tall
Zone 2
White, lacy flowers, spring, followed by red berries; large green leaves, lobes similar to maples; any soil; sun/partial shade; medium water. Best in cool climates.

SERVICEBERRY
Amelanchier spp.
to 20 feet tall
Zone 4
White flower clusters, early spring; purple berries late summer; foliage purplish in spring, green in summer, red in fall; moist soil; sun/partial shade; medium water.

SPIREA
Spiraea spp.
6 feet tall
Zone 4
White or pink flowers, spring; small green leaves turn red in fall; moist, fertile soil; sun/part shade; medium water. Prune and fertilize after flowering.

Colorful Plants for Problem Places

SUN

Full sun and dry soil usually go together. These flowers thrive under scorching conditions, yet bounce back fast after heavy rains.

BLUE FLAX
Linum perenne
2 feet tall
Zone 2
Baby blue flowers, late spring; lacy gray-green foliage. Dry soil, no fertilizer; full sun; extra water only in desert areas.

CALIFORNIA POPPY
Eschscholzia californica
1 foot tall
Zone 6
Orange flowers, spring to fall; lacy green foliage; dry soil, no fertilizer; full sun; water sparingly. Annual or hardy annual.

WATER

Many plants will rot if their roots stay wet for long periods, but some do well in damp soil. Try these plants where soil drainage is slow.

CANNA
Canna **hybrid**
4 feet tall
Zone 7
Red, yellow, or pink flowers, summer, upright stems; long green or variegated leaves. Slightly acidic, moist soil; sun/part shade.

COLEUS
Coleus blumei
3 feet tall
All zones
Blue flowers not as showy as bright foliage; moist, fertile soil; part shade. Annual. Pinch summer blooms to promote bushiness.

WIND

Wind dries out plants quickly and twists their stems, but several tough plants hold up well enough to bring color to windswept spots.

BLACK-EYED SUSAN
Rudbeckia **spp.**
3 feet tall
Zone 3
Bright yellow flowers, summer, with brown or green eyes; hairy green leaves. Any well-drained soil; full sun; occasional water during droughts. Often reseeds.

BLUE FESCUE
Festuca cinerea
1 foot tall
Zone 4
Feathery flower heads; narrow blue-green leaves in clumps; seed spikes, early summer; well-drained soil; full sun; low water.

ALKALINE SOIL

You can modify soil with a high pH by digging in peat moss, leaf mold, or sulfur. Or, simply grow flowers that naturally adapt to alkaline conditions.

BABY'S-BREATH
Gypsophila paniculata
3 feet tall
Zone 3
Airy sprays of white or pink flowers, early summer; narrow green leaves; well-drained neutral to alkaline soil; full sun; occasional water.

CARNATION
Dianthus caryophyllus
hybrids
1-3 feet tall
Zone 7
Pink, white, or red flowers, early summer; gray-green foliage. Well-drained neutral to alkaline soil; full sun; low water.

GAILLARDIA
Gaillardia **spp.**
2 feet tall
Zone 3
Orange-red daisies with yellow petal tips early summer; slightly rough green foliage; dry soil, no fertilizer; full sun; low water. Often reseeds.

PORTULACA
Portulaca grandiflora
8 inches tall
All zones
Red, yellow, pink, and white flowers, summer; semisucculent green foliage; dry soil, moderate fertilizer; full sun; low water. Annual.

YARROW
Achillea filipendulina
3 feet tall
Zone 3
Yellow flowers in flat clusters, summer; finely cut leaves; dry soil, light fertilizer; full sun: occasional water. Good dried flowers.

JAPANESE IRIS
Iris kaempferi
2 feet tall
Zone 4
Purple to marbled pink flowers, late spring; stiff upright leaves; acidic, constantly moist soil; sun/part shade.

MONARDA
Monarda didyma
3 feet tall
Zone 4
Lavender, pink or red flowers, early summer; green foliage; moist, fertile soil; morning sun. Blooms repeat if deadheaded.

SEDGE
Carex **spp.**
1-3 feet tall
Zone 5
Flowers insignificant; reedy grasslike clumps, blue-green foliage; moist soil; sun/light shade; frequent water; some drought tolerance.

PURPLE CONEFLOWER
Echinacea purpurea
3 feet tall
Zone 3
Pinkish-purple flowers, midsummer onward; green foliage; slightly acidic, well-drained soil; full sun; needs little water after first year. Very dependable.

DAFFODIL
Narcissus **hybrid**
18 inches tall
Zone 3
Yellow or white flowers, early spring; strap-like green foliage; well-drained soil enriched with phosphorous; full winter sun; water during active growth.

STONECROP
Sedum spectabile
18 inches tall
Zone 3
Pink flowers late summer to fall; succulent green leaves; well-drained soil; sun/part shade. Can tolerate drought or abundant moisture.

MAIDEN GRASS
Miscanthus sinensis
to 5 feet tall
Zone 5
Silky plumes, late summer into winter; arching leaves form large clumps; any soil; full sun; tolerates damp conditions. Easy to grow.

THRIFT
Armeria maritima
10 inches tall
Zone 5
Pink or white flowers in round clusters spring to summer; stiff grassy foliage forms mat; well-drained to dry, neutral to alkaline soil; full sun.

RED VALERIAN
Centranthus ruber
3 feet tall
Zone 6
Small pink to red flowers, summer; narrow blue-green leaves on stiff stems; any dry, neutral soil; full sun; needs little water. Often reseeds.

Improving Important Spaces

The outdoor spaces that you use most often include entryways, patio or deck, and frequently traveled walkways. Improvements that make these spaces more attractive and useful are good investments with a high return in real-estate value. They also make your yard a more enjoyable place to spend your leisure time.

Landscaping projects for these areas should coordinate logically with the age and style of your house, as well as the character of your neighborhood. Particularly in the front of your house, try to create attractive walkways and entryway plantings that are not radically different from those of your closest neighbors. Since back yards are usually more private, use those spaces to indulge your personal tastes and interests.

When planning projects for entryways and outdoor living areas, keep in mind that the primary purpose of those spaces is to accommodate people. Make walkways as wide as possible, and locate beds where they will not get in the way of your family, guests, and pets. Add lighting where it will make outdoor spaces more usable and safe. Also choose plants that do not require constant maintenance to keep them looking attractive and neat. ❧

Lighting Your Way

Outdoor lighting lets you stroll safely after dark. Light can also help deter prowlers. And, since most people work during the day, lighting greatly expands your opportunities for outdoor living when you come home from work.

To have the intense light needed for a basketball hoop or an outdoor workspace, you can mount spot floodlights on the eaves of your house. A relatively bright light at the front door makes sense for security reasons, but softer lights do a better job of illuminating steps, walkways, and special landscape features. Small, soft lights are easy to hide from direct view among shrubs or near stonework and can be positioned so they won't shine in your eyes. Most home supply stores carry a wide assortment of easy-to-install landscape lights.

Although solar-powered light fixtures are available, most outdoor lighting still runs on electricity connected to the electrical system in your house. Wiring for modest projects, such as lighting for a deck area and steps, can usually be connected to the circuits you already have. However, running an elaborate light system for a large landscape and pool will probably require a new circuit and fuse box. Unless you are skilled at wiring, hire a licensed electrician for this job.

WALKWAY LIGHTING

The steps on a deck can be illuminated with low voltage deck lights mounted flush against the posts that support the steps. Kits that include a power pack, cable, and six or more 7-watt bulbs in weather-resistant fixtures generally cost under $100 and use less electricity than one 60-watt, household light bulb. Study the kit's instructions before you begin the project. If you do not have an outdoor grounded electrical outlet to service your deck lights, have one installed by a licensed electrician. ❧

HAVE ON HAND:

▶ Lighting kit

▶ Tape measure

▶ Small flat head screwdriver

▶ Small Phillips head screwdriver

▶ Pencil

▶ Power drill and ¹⁄₁₆-inch bit

▶ Box of 1-inch cable staples

▶ Hammer

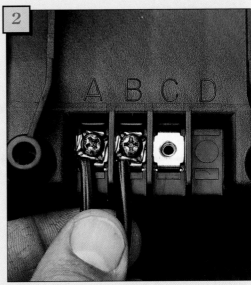

Obtain a suitable kit. Measure the cable's route from nearest outdoor electrical outlet to location of deck lights. Count number of lights desired.

Attach cable wires to power pack from kit according to manufacturer's instructions. Screw connections down tightly.

Hang power pack on the wall within 1 foot of grounded electrical outlet and more than 1 foot above the ground.

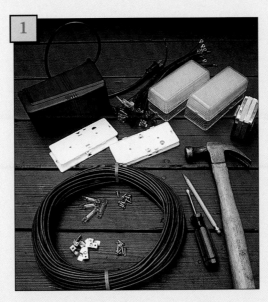

Stretch cable along route where lights will be installed. Leave some slack. Allow 10 feet of cable between power pack and first light.

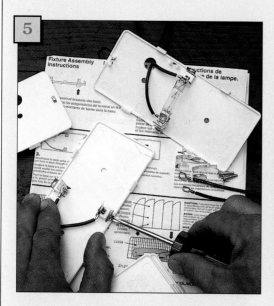

Following manufacturer's directions for lighting fixtures, attach wires to terminal posts or clamps on bases of fixtures. Install bulbs.

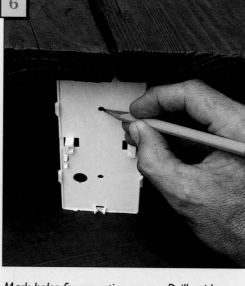

Mark holes for mounting screws. Drill guide holes. Screw bases in desired locations for lights. Snap on light covers.

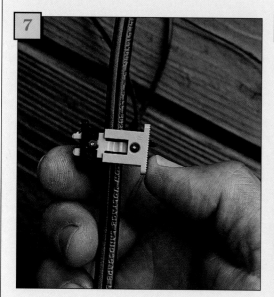

Connect cable to lights according to instructions. Plug in power pack and turn on. Check to see that all lamps light properly.

Secure cable to underside of deck with staples. Do not hit cable with hammer or compress cable with staples. Secure cover on power pack.

HERE'S HOW

UNDERGROUND WIRING

Even if you hire an electrician to install new wiring for outdoor lighting, you can save money by preparing the trenches for buried cables yourself. Buried cables are protected from moisture by a plastic covering, but it's up to you to make sure they will never be sliced by a shovel. Dig trenches 4 inches deep, and cover cables with any rigid material that will not rot, such as strips of fiberglass, PVC pipe, or even an old garden hose, before refilling the trench. Also, record the location of the new wiring on the base plan of your home so that you will always know where you should not dig.

Alternatives

DOWN LIGHTING

Lights that shine down through trees create shadows, transforming your yard into a theatrical scene after dark. White or pastel-colored flowers will appear luminous under downlights, which also are ideal for brightening outdoor dining areas and play spaces.

When using down lighting, you will get better visibility and a more interesting pattern of shadows by installing several lights of different sizes in trees and on buildings or by placing them on posts. Lights that are pointed straight down create an intense circle of light, while those pointed at an angle make an elliptical pattern with longer, more dramatic shadows. Avoid using a single, high-wattage spotlight for down lighting, as it will create a strong contrast between glaring light and very dark shadows that will be difficult for people to navigate.

To find the best down-lighting plan for your yard, experiment with different configurations using ladders, shop lights (or lamps from your house), and extension cords. Try out your ideas, and you will quickly discover that your home landscape has a hitherto unsuspected and new kind of beauty. ❧

UP LIGHTING

Lights installed at or near ground level can add drama to your landscape when used to spotlight centers of interest. Use them to emphasize the shapes of decking, stone walks, garden ornaments, or sculpture. Up lighting is also a great way to define the silhouette of a leafless tree in winter. Frame your yard with uplights set around its boundary so that they reflect off walls or fences, enlarging the scene.

Plan your lighting so there is neither too much nor too little. Light-colored statuary, for example, needs only low-wattage lamps since light colors are reflective. Darker areas, such as a water garden, look best with several lights placed among the stones and plants at the water's edge. They will make the water's surface seem like a black mirror.

When entertaining, add supplemental lighting. The flickering light from oil lamps or candles creates interesting shadows—but be careful not to set them near anything flammable. To guide your guests who wish to stroll along your garden path, use luminarias—candles set in sand-filled, open paper bags. ❧

A Garden for Your Patio

THIS GARDEN THRIVES WITH

SUN
Full

WATER
Low to medium

SOIL
Well drained

The plants you choose for a patio or deck will be seen up close. What better setting for flowers and herbs with small leaves and tiny flowers? This patio garden showcases herbs, which are easy to grow in a well-drained bed. The adjoining brickwork here helps maintain a dry environment for the herb foliage.

Include your favorite culinary herbs so they will be within easy reach of the kitchen. In cold climates you can replant your patio garden with greenhouse-grown herbs every spring. Or, keep small plants of perennial herbs indoors through the winter months by growing them in pots on a sunny window sill. If you are still left with bare spots to fill during the summer, plant them with annual herbs such as basil, dill, or summer savory. Aside from enjoying their taste, fragrance, flowers, and foliage, you can use herbs in flower arrangements.

Avoid using pesticides when growing herbs you will eat, and also be careful when using cleaning products in your patio area. Such products can easily damage herbs and other plants.

This easy garden built into a simple patio (see Installing a Simple Patio, page 26) is adaptable in many ways to suit your specific situation. ❧

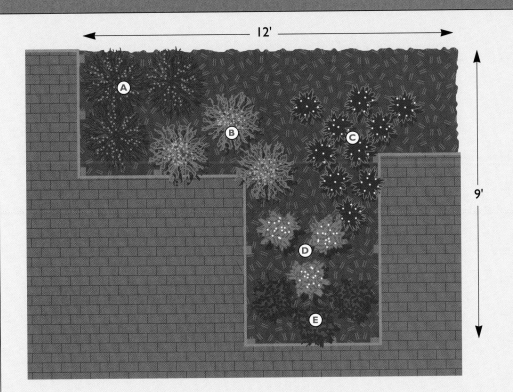

A. English lavender, 3, 2 feet tall

B. Santolina, 3, 2 feet tall

C. Alpine strawberry, 10,
6 inches tall

D. Golden marjoram, 3,
1 foot tall

E. Garden thyme, 3, 8 inches tall

(See next page for more on plants.)

1. To keep your patio free of spilled soil, spread a tarp or an old blanket over the bricks or other patio surface. Reinforce edges of patios made of unmortared bricks with 1 x 4 boards, held in place with wooden stakes. In areas where subterranean termites are common, use recycled plastic lumber or brick as an edging instead of wood.

2. Cultivate the soil in the bed 14 inches deep, and remove 4 inches of loose soil. Use a wheelbarrow to move this excess soil to another part of your yard. If your soil is sandy, work a 4-inch layer of humus into the bed. If your soil type is clay, mix a 2-inch layer of sand and a 2-inch layer of humus into the bed. Rake the bed smooth, mounding the soil slightly in the center if the soil level of the bed is higher than the surrounding patio.

3. Set English lavender (A) and santolina (B) in the rear of the bed, spacing the plants 18 to 24 inches apart to form triangles. Plant alpine strawberries (C) 6 inches apart with their crowns just above the soil line. Plant golden marjoram (D) and thyme (E) in the front, spacing the plants 1 foot apart in a triangular formation.

4. Add individual herb plants you like to open areas in the bed. Water well and mulch lightly.

HERE'S HOW

PROPAGATE HARDY HERBS

You can pot cuttings taken from hardy herbs in late summer and grow them indoors until the following spring. Cut a 4-inch-long piece of stem and remove the leaves from the bottom 2 inches. Plant the cuttings in small pots filled with a sandy potting soil mixture. Keep constantly moist until new growth appears.

Plants for Your Patio Garden

The variations in the foliage, fragrance, and flowers of these plants will keep your patio garden interesting from early spring to late fall. The show begins in spring when the alpine strawberries flower and develop small fruits. Use the fruits whole as garnishes for desserts or beverages or as additions to breakfast cereals or yogurt.

The lavender and santolina are not edible, but swish your hand through their leaves to enjoy their fragrant foliage. You can also cut the stems for fragrant, dried bouquets. The gray-green foliage remains attractive all season long.

The marjoram here is a cousin to oregano, another useful herb for your patio garden. Oreganos and thymes are easy to grow, and their leaves add flavor to many dishes. If cut back in late summer, they often produce a quick flush of new leaves in the fall.

ENGLISH LAVENDER
Lavandula angustifolia
2 feet tall
Zone 5
Lavender-blue flowers, late spring and again in fall; gray-green, needle-like foliage; well-drained, neutral soil; full sun; occasional water.

SANTOLINA
Santolina chamaecyparissus
2 feet tall
Zone 6
Yellow, button-like flowers, summer; tiny, gray-green, fragrant leaves; well-drained, dry soil; full sun; occasional water. Needs little fertilizer.

GOLDEN MARJORAM
Origanum onites 'Aureum'
1 foot tall
Zone 7
White flowers, midsummer; slightly woolly, green-and-yellow variegated leaves with lively pizza flavor; sandy soil; full sun; scant water.

GARDEN THYME
Thymus vulgaris
8 inches tall
Zone 4
Purple flowers, midsummer; small, dark green leaves on stiff stems; well-drained, sandy soil; full sun; occasional water. Needs little fertilizer.

ALPINE STRAWBERRY
Fragaria vesca
6 inches tall
Zone 5
White spring flowers; green leaves with toothed edges; early summer berries; well-drained soil; sun or part shade; occasional water.

CARE FOR YOUR PATIO GARDEN

SPRING Remove mulch. Look for leafy stems sprouting from soil a few inches from last year's plants. Dig and transplant them to pots or to another place in the bed. Fill bare spots with annual herbs after your last frost.

SUMMER Pinch stem tips from marjoram to promote bushiness and delay flowering. Gather and dry leaves from marjoram and thyme. Cut flower stalks from lavender when their color fades to brown. Pull weeds regularly.

FALL Propagate cuttings from hardy herbs. Trim santolina to maintain neat appearance. After hard frost, cut back damaged foliage and pull up annual herbs. Mulch bed lightly to keep soil from washing onto patio.

Alternatives

ACCENT PLANTS FOR PATIO GARDENS

Herbs come in so many different forms, colors, and fragrances that you will never tire of trying new ones in your patio garden. The herbs listed here grow beautifully in well-drained patio beds in many different climates. The grayish foliage of sage and rosemary provides neutral tones to set off more colorful plants. Dwarf curled parsley can be used as an edging around a garden bed or as a dark green accent plant.

Roses are often overlooked as herbs, but as long as they are grown organically you can use the petals to garnish foods and drinks. Try a miniature rose for a small bed, and flank it with low-growing thyme or marjoram. And don't be afraid to let garlic chives into your patio bed. Although the leaves have a distinct onion-garlic flavor, the lovely white flowers carry a faint hint of lilac and bloom in late summer, when many other flowers have come and gone. Many gardeners grow garlic chives for their flowers alone.

If you like to cook or make crafts, you will quickly discover other herbs you will want to grow. Find local herb growers, and let them suggest herbs that grow well in your area.

MINIATURE ROSE 'RISE 'N' SHINE'
Rosa 'Rise 'n' Shine'
22 inches tall
Zone 5
Yellow flowers, early and late summer; small, dark green leaves; well-drained soil; full sun; regular water. Needs light fertilizing spring and midsummer.

GARLIC CHIVE
Allium tuberosum
1-2 feet tall
Zone 5
White, slightly fragrant flowers, late summer; edible, flat, green leaves; well-drained, moist soil; full sun/part shade; regular water. Mulch in winter.

PARSLEY
Petroselinum crispum
1-3 feet tall
Zone 4
White flowers bloom on year-old plants, early summer; dark green, curly, edible leaves; rich, well-drained soil; full sun; provide water during droughts. Grow as an annual.

SAGE
Salvia officinalis 'Tricolor'
2 feet tall
Zone 4
Spikes of fragrant, lavender flowers, midsummer; green-white-and-pink, fuzzy leaves; well-drained soil; sun/part shade; regular water.

ROSEMARY
Rosmarinus officinalis
2-3 feet tall
Zone 7
Light blue flowers, early spring; gray-green, needle-like, edible, fragrant leaves; well-drained, neutral soil; full sun; occasional water.

Enhancing Your Front Walkway

THIS GARDEN THRIVES WITH

SUN
Full to partial

WATER
Medium

SOIL
Average

You can enhance the appearance and value of your property by planting an attractive border in front of your house next to the walkway, where it can be easily admired.

Front walkway beds work best if prominent plants are repeated often to create a clear and continuous pattern of color and texture. Choose flower colors that complement the colors of your house, and use plants that won't litter the walk with fallen leaves, berries, or other debris.

The fragrance of roses is a welcome addition to a walkway border as long as they are planted where their thorny stems won't be a nuisance to people using the walk. In general, steer clear of any shrubs or trees that grow so large they might crowd your windows or shade out neighboring plants. However, a carefully placed small tree, used as an accent, can help dramatize your entry. To keep the walkway from feeling cramped, flank the side of the walkway opposite the bed with lawn grass or a low ground cover, such as creeping juniper. As a finishing touch, bathe the walkway in soft light from fixtures hidden in the bed (see Lighting Your Way, page 102).

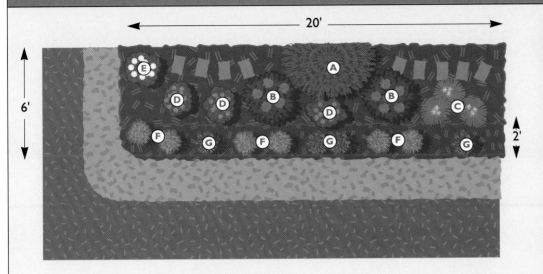

20'

6'

2'

PLANT LIST

A. Japanese black pine,
 1, 15 to 80 feet tall

B. Tree peony, 2, 4 to 6 feet tall

C. Daylily, 3, 2 to 3 feet tall

D. Rose 'The Fairy', 3, 2 to 3 feet tall

E. Rose 'Iceberg', 1, 3 feet tall

F. Blue salvia, 6, 3 feet tall

G. Coral bells, 4, 2 feet tall

(See next page for more on plants.)

1. Plant the pine tree (A) in a hole slightly larger than its rootball. Make sure the pine will not block the view from windows.

2. Before planting tree peonies (B), amend 18-inch-deep planting holes with weed-free compost or humus and set the peonies above the enriched soil. Cover the tops with no more than 2 inches of soil.

3. Plant daylilies (C) in a triangle 4 feet from the peony on the right. Lay stone pavers behind these plants for easy access.

4. Plant 2 'The Fairy' roses (D) on the left in front of the stone pavers and 1 in front of the Japanese pine. Plant the 'Iceberg' rose (E) to the far left as shown. Set pavers to right of 'Iceberg' and behind 'The Fairy'

roses. Dig all planting holes for roses 18 inches deep, and amend the soil with one part bagged humus to three parts soil. Refill holes with 8 inches of amended soil. Spread out rose roots and cover them with 3 inches of soil. Flood with water, then finish refilling the holes.

5. Cultivate a 2-foot-wide strip at the front of the bed. Amend the soil with a 4-inch layer of compost, peat moss, and rotted manure to improve its texture. Rake soil smooth, grading it so that the bed slopes away from the walkway. Plant blue salvias (F) and coral bells (G) in a repetitive pattern. Thoroughly water and mulch the bed.

HERE'S HOW

CREATE A FINISHED LOOK

Mulch the interior of your walkway border to suppress weeds, conserve moisture, and neaten the bed. Define the bed's edges with stone, brick, or landscaping timbers. To keep mulch from spilling into the walkway, use broad stones or make an edging that is slightly higher than the bed itself.

Plants for a Front Walkway

The plants in this walkway border have been arranged to create a dramatic, textured landscape. The Japanese black pine softens the corner of the house and its structure provides interest all year round as a striking visual accent. It adapts well to the pruning it will require in order not to shade the nearby tree peonies. Tree peonies, which like to be left alone, are distanced from areas that require periodic digging, and their taller, mounded forms are complemented by the low-growing shrub roses. The popular white floribunda rose, 'Iceberg', provides an endearing finale on the left.

The diverse plants dominated by the black pine make this bed interesting, yet the orderly repetition of salvias and coral bells along the edge is crucial to its success. They guide the viewer along the walkway, creating a continuous pattern of color and texture. ❧

JAPANESE BLACK PINE
Pinus thunbergiana
15-80 feet tall x 20-40 feet wide
Zone 4
Stiff, 3-inch-long, green needles; brown, 3-inch, oval cones; average soil; full sun; low water. Small pine commonly pruned to desirable size.

TREE PEONY
Paeonia suffruticosa hybrids
3-6 feet tall x 3 feet wide
Zone 4
Pink, white, purple, or yellow flowers up to 1 foot across, summer; broad foliage forms huge mound; moist soil; sun/part shade; medium water.

SHRUB ROSE
Rosa 'The Fairy'
2-3 feet tall
Zone 5
Clusters of small, pink, fragrant roses all summer; well-drained soil; sun/partial afternoon shade; medium water. Easy to grow.

DAYLILY
Hemerocallis hybrids
2-3 feet tall
Zone 3
Yellow, orange, red, or lavender flowers, summer; green, strap-like leaves; average soil; full sun/part shade; low to medium water. Easy to grow.

BLUE SALVIA
Salvia x *superba*
3 feet tall
Zone 5
Violet-purple flower spikes all summer; green foliage; average soil; full sun/part shade; low to medium water. Tolerates drought. Very upright growth habit.

CORAL BELLS
Heuchera sanguinea
2 feet tall
Zone 3
Red-to-salmon flower spikes, early summer; foliage of some cultivars edged with red; moist soil; full sun/part shade; medium water.

CARE FOR YOUR WALKWAY BORDER

SPRING Spread a 2-inch layer of well-composted manure over peonies and beneath roses. Prune roses to remove dead branches and shape the plants. Scatter ¼ cup of 10-10-10 fertilizer per clump over salvias, coral bells, and daylilies. Water.

SUMMER Clip off ragged flowers to keep the border tidy and promote continued bloom. Each rosebush can be fertilized monthly until August; then refresh mulch with bark or pine needles. Pull weeds as they appear.

FALL Dig and divide daylilies and coral bells every third year. After a hard frost, rake up fallen rose leaves and compost if they are healthy. Trim withered branches from peonies. In cold climates, mulch over perennials after the soil freezes. ❧

Alternative

A FRAGRANT FRONT WALKWAY

Back when ladies wore long dresses, it was traditional to edge the front walkway with fragrant plants that would perfume the air when brushed by passing hems and hoops. Planting your walkway border with fragrant plants is still a good idea, for lovely aromas never go out of style.

Plan your fragrant planting so that different perfumes dominate the air at different times. The plants listed below are shrubs and hardy perennials that will take turns scenting the air from spring until fall. These plants release their strongest scents during the day, but some plants give off more perfume at night, including several easy-to-grow annuals. For fragrance after dark, consider adding flowering tobacco, petunias, or a moonflower vine.

Herbs with fragrant foliage and strong forms make wonderful border plants, too. Basils come in a wide variety, including some that are dark purple and others that grow naturally into tight, circular globes. Scented geraniums, especially those that smell of apples and roses, also fit nicely into walkway borders. With these and other scented foliage plants, simply nudge them with your foot or brush them with your hand as you pass by in order to enjoy their perfume. 🍃

DIANTHUS
Dianthus gratianopolitanus '**Bath's Pink**'
10 inches tall
Zone 4
Dainty pink flowers, spring; gray-green foliage forms 4-inch-tall mat; any well-drained soil; full sun to light shade. Tolerates drought.

CREEPING THYME
Thymus praecox ssp. *arcticus,*
4 inches tall
Zone 3
Small white or rose-red flowers, summer; tiny spicy leaves on creeping stems; any soil with excellent drainage; full sun to light shade; water sparingly.

SWEET PEPPERBUSH
Clethra alnifolia
8 feet tall
Zone 3
White or pink flowers looking like bottle brushes midsummer; glossy green leaves; damp, acidic soil; partial shade. Very fragrant.

LILAC
Syringa vulgaris
15 feet tall
Zone 3
Light purple, white, or pink flower clusters, mid-spring; smooth green leaves; alkaline or neutral soil; full morning sun; average water. Very fragrant.

BUTTERFLY BUSH
Buddleia davidii
1 foot tall
Zone 6
Purple, white or pink flower spikes, midsummer to fall on new wood; gray-green foliage; any soil, fertilize yearly in spring; full sun; tolerates drought.

Fashioning a Dooryard Garden

THIS GARDEN THRIVES WITH

SUN
Full to partial shade

WATER
Medium

SOIL
Average

A front door framed with attractive plants is a welcoming sight. One of the most common ways to achieve this warm feeling in a dooryard garden is to use the "funnel effect," gradually narrowing the approach to your house. At the same time, try to keep your front door landing as wide as possible, so that two people can walk to the door side by side.

You will want to make your dooryard beds colorful and interesting without letting the area become cramped. In order to do this—since bed space is usually limited—try using only a few different kinds of plants. Layering them according to height will make the entryway appear elevated. Plants with fine-textured leaves usually work better than broad-leaved plants, which can overpower small spaces.

Match the mood of your house when designing your dooryard garden. Symmetrical layers of plants appear formal, a cottage garden style is more relaxed. Use colorful, low-maintenance annuals in containers or hanging baskets near your entranceway, and change them with the seasons for continuous color. ❦

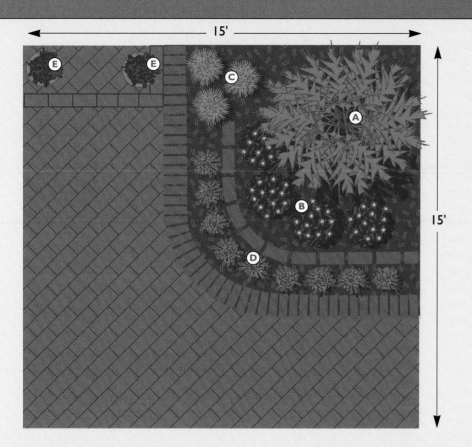

(See next page for more on plants.)

PLANT LIST

A. Tree fern, 1, 20 feet tall

B. Four o'clock, 4, 3 feet tall

C. Mealycup sage, 3, 3 feet tall

D. Rosea ice plant, 9, 6 inches tall

E. Browallia, 2, 18 inches tall

1. Design and finish the hard surfaces of your entryway. Make sure the walkway is firm and comfortable under foot. It should be slightly angled so that rainwater will drain quickly.

2. Amend the soil in dooryard beds with a 4-inch layer of humus. If your soil is clay, also add a 1-inch layer of sand to improve drainage. To create the planting effect shown, rake the cultivated soil into two tiers so that it is 4 inches higher at the top than at the bottom of the bed. If desired, install a row of retaining bricks to hold soil in place.

3. Plant the tree fern (A) 3 feet from the foundation of the house. Cover the root area at the base of the plant with 2 inches of shredded bark or other organic mulch.

4. Plant four o'clocks (B) 15 inches apart near the edge of the top tier of soil. Plant mealycup sage (C) in a tight clump on the entry side of the bed. Edge the front of the bed with rosea ice plants (D), spaced 6 inches apart. Thoroughly water the bed.

5. Install hanging baskets planted with browallia (E). Make sure they are low enough to get ample light, yet widely spaced so they do not block the entryway.

HERE'S HOW

HANGING BASKETS

Hanging baskets are usually suspended from metal hooks screwed into the eaves of the house. To adjust the height of the baskets, attach appropriate lengths of chain between the hooks. Position the baskets slightly above eye level where the bottoms and sides can be clearly seen yet allow you to reach the tops to provide water.

Plants for a Semiformal Garden

The plants in this garden are best suited to warm climates where winter temperatures rarely dip below 20°F. They require water after planting, but once they have developed a strong root system they are moderately tolerant of dry weather conditions. This is a great asset in the dooryard garden, for it means you will not be constantly flooding your front walkway in an attempt to satisfy thirsty plants.

In climates with colder winters, many of the plants featured elsewhere in this book can be used in this design. A simple plan that calls for an accent tree or shrub, a drift of herbaceous perennials, and a small, compact edging plant will make an attractive dooryard garden in any climate.

When planning your garden, be sure to check on how much summer sun the area gets. Depending on the orientation of your house and the amount of shade cast on your dooryard, you may need to include some shade-tolerant plants in your plans. 🌿

TREE FERN
Alsophila tricolor
20 feet tall
Zone 8
No flowers; finely divided, green foliage; well-drained, neutral soil; partial shade, with shelter from hot sun and winter wind; average water.

FOUR O'CLOCK
Mirabilis jalapa
3 feet tall
Zone 7
Red, pink, yellow, or bicolored flowers, summer, close at midday; green leaves; any soil; full sun/part shade; average water. Often reseeds.

MEALYCUP SAGE
Salvia farinacea
3 feet tall
Zone 8
Slender spikes of purple flowers, summer; gray-green leaves; any well-drained soil; full sun/part shade; average water.

ROSEA ICE PLANT
Drosanthemum floribundum
6 inches tall
Zone 8
Pink flowers, late spring and early summer; succulent leaves; any soil; full sun or light shade; requires little water after plants are established.

BROWALLIA
Browallia speciosa
18 inches tall
All zones
Purple flowers, summer; dark green leaves; any good potting soil; partial shade or filtered sun; keep roots moist. Feed monthly in summer.

CARE FOR YOUR DOORYARD GARDEN

SPRING Gather up dead plant debris and fertilize bed with a light application of time-release fertilizer. Renew mulches to suppress weeds and make the bed look neat. Replace plants that were killed during the winter. Install hanging baskets.

SUMMER Pinch leggy stems from browallia to encourage compact, bushy growth. If heavy rains make four o'clocks grow too tall, prune them back by one-third their size. Deadhead spent flowers of mealycup sage to promote repeat blooming.

FALL Trim long stems from rosea ice plant to maintain a clean edge. Allow four o'clocks to die back, and cut off their ragged stems and leaves. Prune browallia and move hanging baskets indoors for the winter. 🌿

Alternative

A CLASSIC COTTAGE GARDEN

If the space outside an informal entryway is too small for a lawn, a colorful cottage garden may be the answer. Historically, cottage gardens of England have included flowers, vegetables, and herbs planted closely together to make the most of the limited space. There is no lawn, and pathways are only wide enough for easy passage. A traditional cottage garden is enclosed by a wooden fence or low stone wall, with a rustic gate to complete the scene.

Flowers for a cottage garden include many old-fashioned annuals, biennials, and perennials, all of which produce brightly colored flowers with little care. Fragrant flowers and those that tend to reseed themselves are favorites, as are edging plants that like to grow alongside pathways paved with stone or brick.

The plants in a cottage garden are seldom planted in rows. Instead, small drifts are allowed to mingle together to form a lush garden full of life and color. Pay attention to bloom times when choosing plants for a cottage garden, for you will want to have different flowers coming in and out of bloom all summer long. Place a garden chair or bench near your entryway so you can enjoy the colorful exuberance of your cottage garden. ❧

HOLLYHOCK
Alcea rosea
5-6 feet tall
All zones
Pink, white, or yellow flowers on tall stalks, early summer; broad, green leaves; any soil; full sun; average water. May grow as annual, biennial, or hardy perennial.

SWEET PEA
Lathyrus odoratus
4 feet tall
All zones
Flowers in most soft colors, early or late summer; green leaves on vining stems that cling with tendrils; fertile, near neutral soil; full sun; average water. Fragrant; grows best in cool weather.

LUPINE
Lupinus hybrids
4 feet tall
All zones
Flowers in many colors and bicolors on upright spikes, early summer; deeply divided green leaves; well-drained, neutral soil; full sun; regular water with light mulch. Usually grows as a short-lived perennial.

FOXGLOVE
Digitalis purpurea
3-4 feet tall
All zones
Purple, white, or yellow flowers on upright spikes, early to midsummer; green leaves; rich, humusy soil; sun/part shade; average water. Biennial in most climates; often reseeds.

SWEET WILLIAM
Dianthus barbatus
6-18 inches tall
All zones
Red, white, pink, or bicolored flowers, early summer; narrow, green leaves; any well-drained soil; full sun or part shade; regular water. Biennial or short-lived perennial; often reseeds.

Accenting Your Landscape

Special features that personalize your landscape can include statuary, a water garden, cozy garden rooms, collections of special plants, or many other design touches that emphasize what you find most satisfying about the world outside your doors. When thinking over creative projects that will become strong visual accents, pursue the ones that will help develop the theme and tone of your landscape. Knot gardens and topiary usually impart a formal feel, while ponds and shady nooks work best in more relaxed, informal settings. Also choose accents that work well with your climate. Where winters are long, features that remain dramatic when shrouded in snow, such as hedges or sculpture, are especially desirable. Where summers are hot, cool shady spots often become favorite garden places. Garden accents can also help attract birds and butterflies to your property, which bring exciting color and motion to any outdoor scene.

Make sure you can easily reach the focal points in your landscape via walkways or mulched paths, and arrange seating so that you and your family can comfortably enjoy these special places. Also consider factors such as street noise and wind when developing a unique niche within your yard. Familiarize yourself with outdoor lighting, which enhances the appeal of many garden accents. ❧

The Allure of Water

Water gardens add a tranquil touch to the landscape, and they are surprisingly easy to build and maintain. Most water gardens include plants and fish, plus a few snails or frogs for added interest. The size of your water garden, which can be as small as a half-barrel, will be determined by a number of factors, including where it will be placed and which features will be included. An ideal depth ranges between 15 and 30 inches, depending on your climate. Make the pond deeper if you live in a very hot or very cold climate so that fish can take cover in the depths during extreme weather.

Ponds larger than 10 x 10 feet usually require a pump to keep the water circulating, but you can also create a small water garden in which plants and fish work together to keep the water in balance (see Here's How, page 122).

Choose a site that can be seen clearly from your house and gets at least the six hours of sun needed daily to keep your aquatic plants healthy. For a more natural effect, add plants around the outside edges. Since visiting your water garden will probably be a daily activity, you may want to include a hard-surfaced or mulched area nearby for a small garden bench or chairs. 🌼

A PREFABRICATED POOL

Rigid fiberglass preformed ponds for water gardens come in many different shapes and depths. Some models are made to be combined into a series of small pools and waterways. This project uses a 3 x 4-foot preformed pond 18 inches deep, which allows enough room for several types of plants and three or four small goldfish or koi. If you run into large rocks or other problems while digging the hole, switch to a flexible plastic liner. Flexible liners cost more than preformed ponds, but they do not require a perfectly excavated hole.

HAVE ON HAND:

▶ One preformed pool

▶ Three 50-pound bags of sand

▶ Tape measure

▶ Shovel

▶ Wheelbarrow

▶ Straight board 4 feet long

▶ Carpenter's level

▶ Stones and plants for landscaping pond edges

Set the pool form on your selected site. Trace around the top rim to define the digging area. Mark the edge with sand.

Dig the hole 1 inch deeper than the depth of the pool. Put excavated soil in a wheelbarrow and move it elsewhere in your yard.

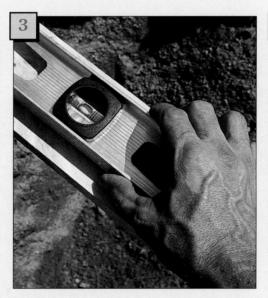

Put a board across the hole and place a carpenter's level on the board. Adjust the soil, making sure the top edges of the hole are level.

Level the bottom of the hole. Set the preformed pond in the hole so that its rim is even with the dirt. Check rim of pond form with the level.

Remove pond form and adjust depth of hole as needed to make the pond rim level. Prepare area around pond for stones and plants.

Spread 1 inch of sand in bottom of hole. Set pond form in hole. Add more sand to support curved edges on bottom of pond form.

Run 4 inches of water into pond. Pack soil to this level behind pond sides. Repeat until pond is full. Place stones and install plants around edges.

Wait three days before introducing aquatic plants. After another week, introduce fish and snails. Expect cloudy water for a few weeks.

HERE'S HOW

CHOOSING AQUATIC PLANTS

You can keep the water in your pond clear and oxygenated by stocking it with a mixture of aquatic plants. In a small water garden, when a pump is not used, at least half of the water's surface should be covered with plants. Floating plants such as water hyacinth, parrot feather, and water lettuce will keep water healthy for fish. (Be aware that water hyacinth is invasive and is not recommended for warmer regions.) Grow water lilies and lotus in submerged pots. Bog or shallow-water plants, such as cattails and rushes, fit nicely on ledges constructed along pond edges.

Alternatives

A SIMPLE FOUNTAIN

A submerged pump can bring the music of falling water to your pond. Pumps with filters also help keep the water clear of excessive algae and debris. You can add a pump after your pond is built. Its output can be piped over stones at the pond's edge to create a waterfall, or you can top the pump with a fountainhead to create bubbling or spraying effects. Check with pond suppliers for equipment that is the right size for your pond.

In a small pond, the turbulence caused by a fountain can disturb aquatic plants, but in larger ponds you can simply place plants around the pond's edges where water movement is slow. Submerged pumps must be set up above the pond's bottom, usually on bricks, so the intake valve does not become clogged with debris. When a pump is run without a filter, you will periodically need to remove the material that accumulates on the screen just outside the intake valve. For safe operation, the pump must be plugged into a moisture-proof outlet with a ground-fault circuit interrupter. This outlet can also be used for outdoor lighting around your pond.

TUB WATER GARDEN

Even if your space is limited, you can make a water garden in a container. You will need a half-barrel, plastic tub, or large fiberglass flowerpot that will hold at least 10 gallons of water and two or three aquatic plants. Most container water gardens can only hold one submerged planting pot, but you can plant a miniature water lily and an upright plant, such as a water iris, together in the same pot. Add a floating plant, and you have a miniature water garden capable of keeping itself in natural balance. A 10-gallon tub garden can also accommodate two small goldfish, called comets.

Without fish to control mosquitoes and other insects, keep water moving in your tub garden by installing an aquarium-sized pump. Make a hole in the bottom of the container large enough for the pump's waterproof electrical cord and plug to pass through. Leaving 6 inches of cord inside the container (and the plug outside), seal the hole around the cord with silicone. When sealant is dry, set the pump above the bottom of the container on bricks. Wood barrels need to be lined with a plastic liner to control seepage. Liners that fit wooden half-barrels are available from water-garden suppliers.

Visually Appealing Verticals

Landscape features that direct the eye upward create drama and excitement and are important parts of the framework, or bones, of a landscape's design. These features, called vertical accents, can make any scene more attractive.

Adding vertical architectural features to your landscape will provide height and varying levels of visual interest. Pergolas and arches improve otherwise bland sites. Tall, potted evergreens placed on either side of an entryway can give the illusion of height. Consider a trellis with fragrant, beautiful roses, a distinctive single specimen tree, or perhaps a free-standing pillar that can support climbing plants. These are some of the best ways to add balance to your landscape's design.

The tall trellis of climbing roses pictured here coaxes the eye upward with its vivid splash of color. However, be careful not to let vertical accents become so overwhelming that your house seems small and squat by comparison. In very small enclosed spaces, a pillar covered with vines will achieve the same effect as this rose-covered trellis. The best vertical features are properly scaled to their site. ✿

INSTALLING A HINGED TRELLIS

A hinged trellis is functional as well as attractive, since it can be moved away to paint the wall or to make pruning a plant less awkward. ❧

HAVE ON HAND:

- ▶ Two 50-inch-long 2 x 2 studs
- ▶ Two 8-foot-long 2 x 4 posts
- ▶ 4 x 6-foot heavy-duty lattice panel
- ▶ Exterior enamel paint and brush
- ▶ Four 2-inch hooks and eyes
- ▶ Pencil
- ▶ Carpenter's level
- ▶ Power drill with wood, masonry bits
- ▶ Four 3-inch lag bolts w/lead anchors
- ▶ $^{7}/_{16}$-inch wrench
- ▶ Screwdriver
- ▶ Saw, power or manual
- ▶ Two 1 $^{1}/_{2}$ x 4-inch strap hinges
- ▶ Posthole digger
- ▶ Two flat stones
- ▶ Hammer
- ▶ Four 1-inch nails
- ▶ Six 1-inch galvanized wood screws
- ▶ 50-pound bag, concrete mix
- ▶ Wheelbarrow
- ▶ Shovel
- ▶ Compost
- ▶ Two climbing roses
- ▶ Mulch
- ▶ Cotton twine or jute

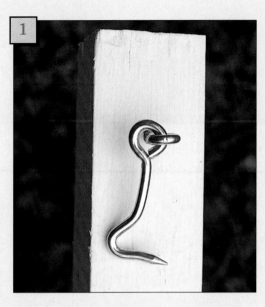

Paint studs, posts, and lattice panel and let them dry. Screw a hook into each stud 1 ½ inches from top and bottom ends.

Mark level horizontal lines on wall 50 inches long, 78 inches and 42 inches from ground. Drill 1-inch holes in wall and studs equally far apart.

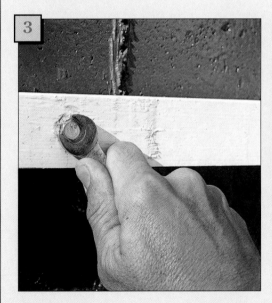

Attach studs to brick wall with lag bolts. Make sure studs are level and ends are plumb before you screw in lag bolts.

Saw off posts 72 inches from tops. Reattach the sawed-off pieces using hinges. Screw eyes on other side of posts 1 inch from top of post.

Dig post holes 20 inches deep. Place flat stones in bottom of holes. Set posts in holes with hinges on the outside. Hook at top to studs.

Adjust posts to make them perfectly plumb. Screw eyes into posts to match hooks in lower horizontal stud. Attach.

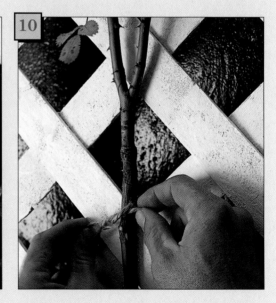

Position lattice panel on posts. Attach panel to posts with four nails. Secure panel to posts with six galvanized wood screws.

Mix concrete with water in wheelbarrow. Fill post holes. Let dry at least 48 hours. Wash wheelbarrow immediately after pouring the concrete.

Dig planting holes for roses at least 18 inches from trellis base. Amend soil with compost. Plant roses and water well. Mulch.

As rose canes grow, tie them to trellis with cotton twine or jute. As you tie, allow room for the stems to thicken.

Alternatives

A SINGLE TREE

Professionally designed home landscapes tend to have one thing in common—a small- to medium-sized ornamental tree placed a few yards from a front corner of the house. It may act as the vertical anchor for a large bed of low-growing shrubs, or it may stand by itself in the lawn. If the tree's purpose is to emphasize the vertical lines of a two-story house, it is usually narrow and tall, such as a column-shaped juniper. In the landscape of a ranch-style house, the tree is more likely to have branches that spread sideways into layers, as do dogwoods and Japanese maples. Flowering cherry, crab apple, and pear trees often are used as vertical accents, too. The best ornamental trees offer something extra in terms of form, flower, fruit for birds or people, or bold fall color.

If your yard is a size that will accommodate only one tree, make the most of it. Surround your tree with a grouping of dwarf shrubs and perennials, or perhaps a blooming ground cover. Finish with a border of edging plants, stonework, or a brick mowing strip. ❧

A PILLAR

Vertical accents that are scaled down to fit small spaces are often called pillars. They function the same as larger vertical structures by making the eye stretch upward while giving the scene more depth. Because the entryway may be the first thing a visitor sees of your yard or landscape, pillars present a great opportunity to refocus attention there.

Gateposts, with or without an attached gate or fence, are classic pillars for defining the entry to a home. In small city yards, the gateposts can be painted to match the front door, which unifies the two elements. Along the entry to a rural property, large stone pillars make a strong statement in the wide-open spaces.

In suburban settings, vertical accents for your entryway might include tall concrete urns spilling over with petunias or verbena, or a pair of tight evergreen shrubs shaped like columns. Single, column-shaped shrubs can become vertical anchors in beds too small to accommodate a tree. In a bed that borders your driveway, use a lamppost as a pillar that also provides outdoor lighting. A birdbath on a thick concrete stand or a bird feeder on a straight black post make attractive, functional vertical accents for your backyard. ❧

Planting a Knot Garden

THIS GARDEN THRIVES WITH

SUN	WATER	SOIL
Full	Moderate	Very well drained

If your taste tends toward the intricate and refined, sculpting selected plants into shapes and patterns can be tremendously satisfying. Knot gardens, topiary, and espalier were invented to be special features in European "pleasure gardens" in centuries past. All are garden elements that look best in formal landscapes where bold symmetrical lines have been incorporated into the design. Swaths of manicured lawn or handsome stonework make perfect matches for these living sculptures.

Knot gardens emphasize pattern and texture and are best located where they can be viewed from above. You might place a sundial, birdbath, or other ornament in the center, where it will be especially visible in winter when the pattern of your knot is outlined in snow.

The steps at right show the traditional way to mark and plant a knot garden, but there is a modern twist you might consider. If you expect persistent weeds to be a problem, cover the prepared soil with landscaping cloth or fabric weed barrier, and bury the outside edges. Mark the pattern on the fabric mulch, and cut x-shaped holes for your plants. Cover the fabric with a decorative mulch when you are finished. 🌿

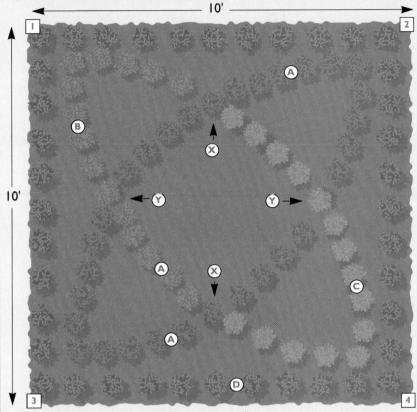

10'

10'

PLANT LIST

A. Germander, 30, 15 inches tall

B. Green santolina, 15, 22 inches tall

C. Silver santolina, 15, 22 inches tall

D. Dwarf Korean boxwood, 40, 2 feet tall

(See next page for more on plants.)

HERE'S HOW

ADDING GARDEN EDGING

You can play up the formal character of your knot garden and make it easier to groom by surrounding it with a brick edging. Dig a trench as deep and wide as your bricks. Level the bottom with ½ inch of sand, set bricks in place, and fill crevices with additional sand.

1. Measure a 10 x 10-foot-square site. Cultivate soil, remove weeds, add soil amendments as needed, and rake smooth.

2. Drive 1-foot stakes into the ground at corners and center. Check measurements to make sure you have a perfect square. The distances between diagonal corners should be the same.

3. Tie taut string between corner stakes. Fill an empty milk jug with dry sand. Mark the line under the string with the sand.

4. Tie one end of a 10-foot length of twine to stake at corner 1, and the other end to the handle of the jug filled with sand. Mark an arc with sand between corner 2 and corner 3. Swing arcs from other corners to form ellipses.

5. Plant the ellipses by placing plants 9 inches apart on the sand line. Where ellipses cross, place plants to create an over-and-under effect. Make the germanders (A) a continuous line at the X points. Use the santolinas (B and C) in a line at the Y points, which will break the line of germanders.

6. Plant boxwoods (D) 10 inches apart on the perimeter sand line. Remove stakes and strings, and water all plants thoroughly. Mulch the spaces inside the pattern with 3 to 4 inches of mulch.

7. When the interior plants show new growth, shear them to a uniform height. Shear boxwoods in midsummer so new growth will harden off before winter.

Plants for a Knot Garden

The plants in this knot garden grow to similar heights, have slight variations in foliage color, and respond well to the uniform clipping needed to make the knot look neat and well groomed. You can shape the tops of the boxwoods into a square if you like, but the interior plants will work best if trimmed to a more mounded form. Electric hedge trimmers will make quick work of this trimming.

It will take two or three years for your knot garden to mature fully. In the first year, trim plants to a uniform height after they show new growth. Be bold about clipping off flower buds, for your goal is to help the plants develop bushy lateral branches rather than flowers. Use a stick marked with the desired height as a guide when pruning. If you like, plant the pockets inside the pattern with annual flowers for extra summer color. ❦

DWARF KOREAN BOXWOOD
Buxus koreana
2 feet tall
Zone 4
Flowers inconspicuous; small evergreen leaves dense and shiny; neutral to slightly acidic soil; sun or part shade. Mulch to protect shallow roots from drought.

GREEN SANTOLINA
Santolina virens
22 inches tall
Zone 5
Greenish yellow rounded flowers, summer; lacy green fragrant foliage; any soil, needs little fertilizer; full sun; occasional water during droughts.

SILVER SANTOLINA
Santolina chamaecyparissus
22 inches tall
Zone 5
Small yellow button flowers, summer; frosty, gray-green, fragrant leaves; any well-drained, dry soil, little fertilizer; full sun.

GERMANDER
Teucrium chamaedrys
15 inches tall
Zone 5
Rose-pink flowers, summer; glossy green fragrant leaves with gray undersides; tolerates poor, rocky soil; full sun; little water.

CARE FOR YOUR KNOT GARDEN

SPRING Remove weeds and fertilize plants by scratching 10-10-10 fertilizer into the soil above plant roots. Use half the recommended application rate. Trim off all dead branches and replace any plants killed during the winter. Renew mulch.

SUMMER When new growth becomes thick, prune plants to shape them and promote bushiness. Contour boxwoods. Prune to limit flowering since it weakens the foliage. Provide water if soil becomes very dry, but avoid wetting the foliage.

FALL Remove weeds and pull up any annuals. Lightly trim wayward branches and renew mulches. If your knot garden will receive strong winter winds, surround it with a windbreak of burlap hung between stakes at each corner. ❦

Alternative

TOPIARY AND ESPALIER

Topiary and espalier involve training and pruning plants to rigid shapes. Such highly disciplined plants fit best in formal settings. Topiaries include freestanding shrubs trained and pruned into geometric shapes, as well as whimsical animals shaped out of chicken wire, which are stuffed with sphagnum moss and clothed in vines such as English ivy or wintercreeper. Topiary is usually placed in high visibility areas as a decorative landscape accent.

Espalier can turn a plain wall into a work of art. In this type of living sculpture, the young limbs of trees or vines are pinned or tied to a wall or trellis in a symmetrical pattern. When the pattern is achieved, regular pruning keeps the plant properly shaped. Many fruit trees can be trained into lovely espaliers that also bear fruit. Crab apples are a good choice for beginners. You can experiment with espaliered vines by working with annual vines first and then switching to a perennial vine when you're ready for a permanent espaliered accent. ❦

ENGLISH YEW
Taxus baccata
25-40 feet tall
Zone 3
Flowers insignificant; glossy, dark green needles; female plants develop red berries, late summer; any near-neutral soil; full sun/part shade; average water.

ENGLISH BOXWOOD
Buxus sempervirens
6 feet tall
Zone 6
Inconspicuous flowers; small, bright green glossy leaves on woody branches; neutral to slightly acidic moist soil; full sun/part shade. Mulch well.

WINTERCREEPER
Euonymus fortunei var. *radicans*
15 feet tall
Zone 5
Inconspicuous flowers; dark green glossy leaves with toothed edges, vining habit; slightly acidic soil, little fertilizer; full sun/part shade; occasional water.

FIRETHORN
Pyracantha fortuneana
10 feet tall
Zone 6
Small white flowers, spring; glossy green leaves, slightly thorny stems; orange-red berries ,fall to winter; any good soil; full sun; avoid heavy watering.

CRABAPPLE
Malus 'Dolgo'
30 feet tall
Zone 4
Showy white blossoms, early spring; dense, reddish green foliage; clusters of edible red fruits, late summer; neutral fertile soil; full sun; average water.

Creating Enclosures

THIS GARDEN THRIVES WITH

SUN	WATER	SOIL
Part shade	Regular to high	High organic matter

There are few outdoor areas more inviting than an enclosed garden designed for comfort and coziness. Whether its walls are made of plants, fencing, or stone, an enclosed garden space provides a tranquil oasis from everyday noise and activity. To adults, garden enclosures are private spots for reading, reflecting, and resting. To children, outdoor rooms are secret places that set the stage for hours of creative play.

When planning your enclosed space, think about what the site has to offer and what you will do in the space once it is complete. Decide what kind of seating, tables, or other furnishings you want to have and sketch a floor plan in the same way that you would if you were creating an indoor room.

To make your enclosure more livable, pave the ground with pebbles, gravel, or other clean mulch material. Whether you are opening up a wooded spot or creating an enclosure in a sunny area, leave one side open to keep it from feeling cramped.

Since you will probably want to use your outdoor room as a place to relax, you may want to choose plants that require little care or cleanup. Most of the plants in the design for this enclosure are permanent and require minimal attention. ❧

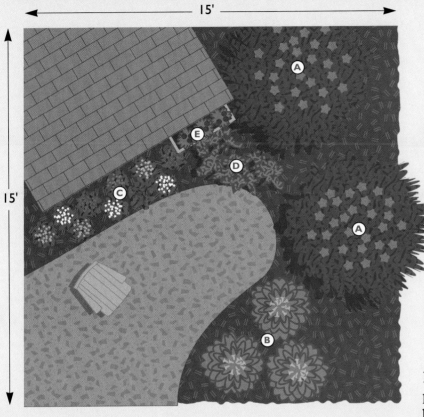

15'

15'

A. Rhododendron, 2, 2 to 12 feet tall

B. Hosta, 3, 3 feet tall

C. Impatiens, 9, 14 inches tall

D. Variegated English ivy, 8,

   30 feet long

E. Zonal geranium, 3, 1 to 2 feet tall

(See next page for more on plants.)

soil. Set the plants high in the planting holes so that the roots are barely covered. Water well and mulch with pine needles, shredded bark, or leaf mold.

4. Amend planting holes, then plant two hostas (B) 14 inches from edge of walkway, with a third offset behind the two, as shown.

1. Remove plants from the woodland area where you want your enclosure. As you dig, mark natural planting holes you find between large tree roots. Prune low limbs from shade trees.

2. Define your walkway and plan placement of furniture. Add or shift topsoil as needed to create level space for furniture. Grade walkway into a slight slope, so rainwater will run off rather than form muddy puddles. Pave open area with a 2-inch layer of pebbles or gravel.

3. Plant rhododendrons (A) in planting holes that have been amended with one part peat moss to three parts

5. Work amendments into area to be planted with impatiens and ivy, or set up a shallow raised bed and fill it with humus-rich soil that holds moisture well. Plant impatiens (C) and variegated ivy (D) and mulch.

6. Plant geraniums (E) in manger planter or wall basket, along with a few rooted pieces of variegated ivy.

7. Water thoroughly. Set furniture in place.

HERE'S HOW

INSTALLING A PLANTER

Wall baskets and manger planters come with burlap or moss liners to prevent loss of potting soil. While you are installing the hanging hardware for your planter, soak the liner in a bucket of water. Fit the wet liner into the planter and fill with potting soil and plants after the planter is in place.

Plants for a Shady Garden Room

This garden room has a roof provided by the canopies of nearby shade trees. With low tree limbs trimmed off to admit shade from high limbs, the plants beneath benefit from plenty of filtered light and fresh air. High shade is a desirable natural light since it accommodates both sun and shade plants. Rhododendrons and hostas are usually regarded as shade plants, yet they show strong growth in partial high shade. Geraniums prefer full sun but can grow quite well in the dappled light beneath tall deciduous trees.

When choosing a rhododendron, check with local nurseries for recommended cultivars. There are many species and unique hybrids to choose from with varying tolerances to cold and heat. You will also want to plan for the eventual height of those you choose. ❧

RHODODENDRON
Rhododendron spp.
2-12 feet tall
Zone 4
Red, white, pink, or yellow flower clusters, spring; leathery, evergreen leaves; acidic, moist soil; partial shade.

HOSTA 'SHADE MASTER'
Hosta undulata
3 feet tall
Zone 3
Lavender flowers on tall stalks, midsummer; broad, wavy, lime-green leaves; fertile soil; shade; regular water. May not bloom in deep shade.

VARIEGATED ENGLISH IVY
Hedera helix 'Argenteo-variegata'
to 30 feet long
Zone 5
Green-and-white leaves with pointed lobes on almost woody stems; tolerates acidic soil; needs more shade than nonvariegated form; average water.

IMPATIENS
Impatiens wallerana hybrids
14 inches tall
All zones
Flowers in many colors, all summer; dark green leaves, succulent stems; fertilize monthly; partial shade; copious water.

ZONAL GERANIUM
Pelargonium x hortorum
1 to 2 feet tall
All zones
Red, white, or rose flower clusters; green or variegated leaves show dark halo in cool weather; any soil, light summer fertilizer; sun or part shade; avoid overwatering.

CARE FOR YOUR GARDEN ROOM

SPRING Gather up fallen tree limbs and other debris. Mulch beneath rhododendrons and hostas with pine needles or shredded leaves. Plant impatiens and geraniums. Divide and replant new, rooted pieces of ivy.

SUMMER Add water soluble fertilizer once a week to the water used for geraniums and impatiens. Impatiens need abundant water, but geraniums like their roots slightly dry. Cut flower spikes off hostas when blossoms fade, to encourage leaf growth.

FALL Gather fallen leaves and add to compost pile. Pull up dead impatiens and geraniums and compost healthy plant debris. Mulch around the rhododendrons. After frost, clip the foliage from hostas. If desirable, divide and replant hostas. ❧

Alternative

EVERGREEN ENCLOSURES IN FULL SUN

You can use hedges, trees, fences, or a combination of these elements to create an enclosed space in a sunny, open area. Panels of fence will work well for one of your walls provided you already have similar fencing placed in other parts of your yard. Fences that repeat within the landscape look more at home than short runs of fencing that stand alone.

Hedging is a powerful way to enclose space, so use a hedge for only one or two sides of your outdoor room. Consider installing a hedge for the enclosure's back wall, planting two small trees for the adjoining side walls, and leaving the side opposite the hedge open. This enclosure can be made large enough for a dining table, or you can furnish it with a hammock, swing, or a small grouping of table and chairs and/or a chaise.

Choose plants for hedging that are properly scaled to your site. Very large hedges will make a small yard seem smaller, just as tiny hedges will be lost in a large space. For a formal look, use a single line of hedge shrubs. You can achieve a more casual look if you combine traditional hedge plants with low shrubs to create a more natural, layered appearance. ❧

HOLLY 'NELLIE R. STEVENS'
Ilex x. 'Nellie R. Stevens'
10 feet tall
Zone 6
Greenish white flowers, spring; glossy evergreen spine-tipped leaves; average soil; full sun; moderate water .Bright red berries, spring; male plant needed for pollination.

UPRIGHT JUNIPER
Juniperus chinensis
6-20 feet tall
Zone 4
Flowers insignificant; dark green needle-like foliage, many sizes and forms; near-neutral soil, light fertilizer in spring; full sun; average water.

MYRTLE
Myrtus communis
8 feet tall
Zone 7
White flowers, spring, followed by black berries; glossy leaves fragrant when crushed; neutral to acidic soil; full sun or part shade; average water.

ENGLISH YEW
Taxus baccata
4-15 feet tall
Zone 4
Flowers insignificant; dense, dark green, needle-like leaves on spreading branches; any neutral to acidic soil; sun to part shade; average water.

DWARF EASTERN HEMLOCK
Tsuga canadensis cultivars
10 feet tall
Zone 4
Flowers insignificant; light-textured needled leaves on spreading branches; any slightly acidic soil; full sun; supplemental water generally not required.

Glossary

ACID (acidic) a soil with a pH lower than 7.0. Slightly acidic soil is acceptable to most plants. A soil pH below 5.5 is too acidic for many plants.

ALKALINE a soil with a pH higher than 7.0; opposite of acidic soil. Also known as sweet soil.

ANNUAL a plant that sprouts from seed, grows, flowers, sets seed, and dies within one year.

BARK MULCH a material sold in bags, made from tree bark that is stripped from logs at lumber mills. The size of the bark varies between large nuggets and small chips.

BICOLOR a blossom in which petals are marked with two colors, as when pansies have dark blotches, or petunias have white petals edged with purple.

BIENNIAL a plant that begins growth one year and flowers, sets seed, and dies after living through one winter.

CLAY a soil type made up of very small soil particles. Clay soils easily become hard and compacted, and may not drain well unless they are improved by adding organic matter.

COMPOST the soft organic material that results from the decaying of plant and animal matter.

CROWN the point where leaves emerge from a plant, just above the place where roots are joined to aboveground plant parts.

CULTIVAR a strain of a plant that has been selected and propagated vegetatively, from rooted cuttings or root divisions, rather than by seeds.

DECIDUOUS a plant that drops its leaves in fall and produces new foliage in spring.

DIVISION the technique of separating plant clumps into several smaller parts by pulling or cutting apart crowded roots, bulbs, or corms.

DORMANT the "resting" state of a plant, as when perennials die back in winter.

DRAINAGE the gradual flow of water through soil. Drainage depends on steepness of slope, type of soil, and factors such as compaction.

EROSION the movement of topsoil away from a given site by water or wind.

EVERGREEN a plant that holds its green foliage through winter, and never has bare branches.

FORMAL in garden design, a style that is clearly structured by defined lines, and shows a high degree of symmetry and balance. The overall mood of a formal landscape is very neat and orderly. Front yards usually involve formal designs.

FOUNDATION the part of a house that rests upon the ground, or extends into the ground. The foundation is usually constructed of concrete or concrete blocks.

FRAMING definition of a landscape view by the creation of visual boundaries with plantings or structures.

GRADE a term that describes the degree of slope in a given site. Level sites have zero grade. To grade a site means to reshape soil into a very slight slope that helps water drain away from the house.

GROUND COVER any plants, shrubs or materials planted or placed where grass is not desired or practical. Used to cover steep slopes or rocky terrains, for example.

HARDY describes a plant that survives winter, either in a dormant state or while holding green leaves.

HUMUS decayed organic matter that is added to soil to improve its structure and ability to hold air and water. Compost, peat moss, rotted leaves, weathered straw, composted bark, and rotted sawdust are different types of humus.

HYBRID a genetically unique variety created by crossing specific parents. Hybrid varieties often are unusually vigorous and resistant to pests or diseases. The seeds produced by hybrid plants often show characteristics of the parent varieties rather than the unique hybrid.

INFORMAL in garden design, a style that often shows loose, curved lines rather than straight ones, makes use of plants in their natural shapes, and imparts a mood of lush exuberance. Backyards often reflect informal designs.

LANDSCAPE DESIGN the purposeful layout of plants, shrubs, trees, structures and ornaments in outdoor areas.

LEVEL in carpentry, a board, plank, or other structural part that is perfectly horizontal. A tool called a carpenter's level is used to see if the line is perfectly horizontal.

LIME a calcium compound usually applied to acidic soil to raise the pH into the normal range. The type of lime best for gardens, called agricultural or garden lime, is made from ground limestone.

MICROCLIMATE an area within a larger climate in which local factors such as shade, moisture and exposure make it different from the surrounding area.

MULCH any material spread over the soil surface to retain soil moisture, moderate soil temperature, and suppress the growth of weeds.

NEUTRALS in garden design, neutral plants are those with gray or gray-green foliage, or sometimes plants that bear white flowers. Neutrals are used to offset potential clashes between different colors, to bridge the visual gap between textures, or to impart a feeling of spaciousness.

PANICLE the plant structure that works like a flower spike in grasses. Although not true flowers, panicles produce pollen and later develop seeds.

PAVERS special bricks or flat pieces of formed concrete used for constructing walkways. Pavers are usually not as thick as building bricks, and are made of a dense material so that they resist cracking under pressure.

PEAT MOSS a type of humus made from pulverized peat, a bog plant that grows in scattered cold climate areas. Peat moss has an acidic pH.

PERENNIAL a plant that can live for more than two years.

PESTICIDE a substance used to kill insects, control diseases, or both. Systemic pesticides are taken up by plants and become part of their physiology; they are not used on edible plants. The label on any pesticide product shows a specific list of plants on which the product may be used. Types of pesticides include insecticides, which control only insects, and fungicides, which control fungal diseases.

pH a measure of a soil's acidity or alkalinity on a scale of 1.0 to 14.0, with 7.0 being neutral. A pH below 5.5 is acidic; 6.0 is slightly acidic; above 7.0 is alkaline.

PLUMB in carpentry, a post or plank that is perfectly vertical.

PRUNING the process of cutting away unwanted branches from a plant. Pruning can be done to remove damaged or diseased plant parts, to shape the plant, or to force the plant to send available energy to flowering buds.

REPETITION a design term that describes the use of certain plants or plant combinations in a repeating pattern within the landscape.

RESEED the ability of some plants to shed seeds that successfully germinate and grow.

ROOTBALL the mass of roots and potting soil visible when you remove a plant from its pot.

SAND a soil type made up of large, gritty soil particles. Sandy soils drain quickly and do not hold moisture well unless they are improved by the addition of humus.

SOIL HEAVING the forcing of plants, stones, or other materials to the soil surface through alternate freezing and thawing. Affects young plants in particular .

TENDER a plant susceptible to frost damage.

TOP DRESSING adding compost or fertilizer to the soil surface above plant roots.

VERTICAL ACCENT any upright plant (including trees, shrubs, vines, grasses) or structure used as a contrast or focal point in the landscape.

Index

TIME® LIFE BOOKS

Time-Life Books is a division of Time Life Inc.

TIME LIFE INC.

CHAIRMAN AND CEO	Jim Nelson
PRESIDENT AND COO	Steven L. Janas

TIME-LIFE TRADE PUBLISHING

VICE PRESIDENT AND PUBLISHER	Neil Levin
Senior Director of Acquisitions and Editorial Resources	Jennifer Pearce
Director of New Product Development	Carolyn Clark
Director of Marketing	Inger Forland
Director of Trade Sales	Dana Hobson
Director of Custom Publishing	John Lalor
Director of Special Markets	Robert Lombardi
Director of Design	Kate L. McConnell

LANDSCAPING PROJECTS

Managing Editor	Donia Ann Steele
Project Manager	Jennifer Pearce
Consulting Editor	Linda B. Bellamy
Production Manager	Carolyn Mills Bounds
Quality Assurance Manager	Miriam P. Newton
Technical Specialist	Monika Lynde
Reprint Coordinator	Jennifer L. Ward
Quality Assurance (reprint)	Jim King, Stacy L. Eddy

Produced by Storey Communications, Inc.
Pownal, Vermont

President	M. John Storey
Executive Vice President	Martha M. Storey
Vice President and Publisher	Pamela B. Art
Director of Custom Publishing	Amanda Haar
Project Manager	Vivienne Jaffe
Book Design	Jonathon Nix/Verso Design
Design and Layout	Mark Tomasi
Design Assistant	Jennifer Jepson
Editing	Joan Burns
Author	Barbara Pleasant
Primary Photography	A. Blake Gardner

Additional photography: Henry W. Art; Cathy Wilkinson Barash; Kim Blaxland/PN; Pat Bruno/PI; Gay Bumgarner; Karen Bussolini/PI; © Crandall & Crandall; R. Todd Davis; Alan and Linda Detrick; Thomas Eltzroth; Derek Fell; Peggy Fisher; Roger Foley; David Goldberg; Harry Haralambou/PI; Saxon Holt; Jerry Howard/PI; Bill Johnson; Peter Lindtner; Robert Lyons; Charles Mann; J. Paul Moore; Karin O'Connor; Jerry Pavia; Pam Peirce; Paul Rocheleau; Richard Shiell; Albert Squillace/PI; Patricia Taylor; Michael S. Thompson; Chuck Weight; judywhite.

Cover photography: A. Blake Gardner and J. Paul Moore.

Pre-Press Services, Time-Life Imaging Center
Printed in U.S.A.
10 9 8 7 6 5 4 3

TIME-LIFE is a trademark of Time Warner Inc. and affiliated companies.
Time-Life How-To is a trademark of Time-Life Books.

Library of Congress Cataloging-in-Publication Data
Time-Life how-to landscaping projects : simple steps to enhance your home and yard.
    p.   cm.
    Includes index.
    ISBN 0-7835-4867-2
    1. Landscape gardening.   I. Time-Life Books
SB473.T58 1997   96-34320
712—dc20   CIP

Books produced by Time-Life Trade Publishing are available at special bulk discount for promotional and premium use. Custom adaptations can also be created to meet your specific marketing goals. Call 1-800-323-5255.

Zone Map

ALASKA

HAWAII

Range of Average Annual Minimum
Temperatures for Each Zone

Zone 1	Below -50° F
Zone 2	-50° to -40° F
Zone 3	-40° to -30° F
Zone 4	-30° to -20° F
Zone 5	-20° to -10° F
Zone 6	-10° to 0° F
Zone 7	10° to 20° F
Zone 8	20° to 30° F
Zone 9	30° to 40° F
Zone 10	40° to 50° F
Zone 11	50° to 60° F